Based between the US and Australia, Natasha Oakley is a pioneer Super Influencer with over 3.6 million followers, and a leading voice in the social media space.

She and her best friend, Devin Brugman, set up 'A Bikini A Day' in 2012 as an outlet to share their favourite swimwear, which quickly took off as one of the most well-renowned marketing platforms in the industry. The huge success saw the pair co-found their own swimwear label, Monday Swimwear, in 2014, which created worldwide recognition for the duo, not only as role models, but successful businesswomen. Recently, in 2023, the pair expanded their portfolio with the launch of Monday Body, focusing on eco-friendly activewear and every-day essentials. These days, Natasha counts Model, Presenter, Designer, Producer, Entrepreneur, CEO and Digital Influencer among her credits.

In 2020, Natasha also co-founded, and is the CEO of, The Pilates Class, a highly successful online fitness platform, generating a revenue in the multi-millions and becoming one of the most internationally recognised online Pilates classes within twelve months of launching. Tash's booming businesses truly are a testament to her entrepreneurial spirit.

EXCESSIVELY OBSESSED

Find your passion, build your business,
learn your limits, love your life

Natasha Oakley

PIATKUS

PIATKUS

First published in Great Britain in 2024 by Piatkus

1 3 5 7 9 10 8 6 4 2

A CIP catalogue record for this book
is available from the British Library.

ISBN: 978-0-349-43792-7

Typeset in Sabon by M Rules
Printed and bound in Great Britain by Clays Ltd, Elcograf S.p.A.

Papers used by Piatkus are from well-managed forests
and other responsible sources.

Piatkus
An imprint of
Little, Brown Book Group
Carmelite House
50 Victoria Embankment
London EC4Y 0DZ

An Hachette UK Company
www.hachette.co.uk

www.littlebrown.co.uk

To Sophia and Fleur
I hope you know the world is your oyster and you can soar
to unimaginable heights ... if you just believe you will and
work damn hard.

Contents

Part 4 Finding fulfilment, avoiding burnout

Introduction

I've been obsessed with being in business for as long as I can remember. But not just being in business – *running* a business.

You might say I came by it naturally. In 1980, ten years before I was born, my mother won the title Miss Australia. Immediately upon winning, she opened her own real estate agency. Some beauty queens at the time went into full-time modelling or acting or charity work – my mother went into business. My dad, a championship surfer, works as a private investigator and owns his own company too. They split up when I was five years old, but I grew up watching both of them run their own small businesses and create their own success, and I knew from an early age that I wanted to do the same.

Back then, I would go to my mother's office most days after school and sit at the reception desk, stamping and stapling documents and shuffling papers around just to feel like I was a part of things. I felt so important! To me that's what being an entrepreneur was all about. Getting things done and earning a sense of independence and success – even back then I felt like I was in my purpose when I was 'doing business'. There was a charged energy that ran through me as I sat behind that front desk. As far as I was concerned there was nothing cooler, and nothing more fun, than being a Business Woman. It was the ultimate dream.

I never had any illusions about how much effort it would take to one day find the success I craved. My mom worked six days a week, my dad worked all hours of the day – I was exposed early to what it takes to make it as an entrepreneur, and I was ready.

No big surprise, then, that the moment I could try to sell something, I was out there hustling. I was the six-year-old selling rocks to neighbours; the ten-year-old making custom Christmas cards that had a single scribble across the front and selling them to family friends for $20 a pop (very pricey cards). In high school, I loved taking art class and eventually started making large-scale paintings, some of which I sold for $1,000! (Consider that my first lesson in knowing your worth and charging accordingly.)

Between primary and high school, I went to *nine* different schools, because my family moved around a lot due to my parents' jobs. Some people might have hated that – it certainly made it hard to get too settled in – but it was a huge lesson for me in adaptability and weathering change. In high school, I was a pretty good student. From the very beginning I excelled and topped my year in the subjects I cared about (business, art, English) but those I didn't (maths, science) were a totally different story. From a young age, passion was what drove my achievement.

In Australia, you have to be fourteen years and nine months to get a job, and the moment I was of age, I was tracking down work. My first proper employment was in a bakery, and while making bread and serving pastries wasn't my destiny, I loved that job because it was my first taste of financial freedom and independence. I relished having the ability to do what I wanted to do and buy what I wanted to buy without having to rely on anyone else. My mom always talked up the importance of independence and the value of being able to rely on yourself, and I took her message seriously. I took one job after another – the bakery was first, but I also worked at a printing company, Bang-On T-Shirts, and in basically every retail position at our local Westfield mall. I was a Red Bull girl at one point, and at many times I held two jobs simultaneously. But no matter what job I was in, I had the same goal: kill the game. I wasn't trying to bide my time and cash a cheque, I was trying to be the best. If there was any sort of commission – or any kind of information on who had the best sales, even if it didn't come with a financial incentive – I was checking those rankings every hour. I wanted to be the best at whatever I was doing. That's not because I felt like I was in a competition or wanted to 'beat' anyone (other than myself) but because if I'm spending my time on something, I commit. I work hard and want to keep improving. I'm ambitious, and I don't feel like myself if I'm not pouring myself into a project. So I didn't care what the assignment was, or if I loved it or hated it. It didn't matter if I was selling T-shirts or serving drinks. If it was my job, I was going to excel.

As I grew up and moved around and tried to figure out what my life should look like as an adult, the one constant was that work ethic. But it wasn't just that I was a hard worker or honoured my commitments, I actually really loved putting in my time and earning my keep and learning how to navigate different businesses and different roles. I strongly believe that there is no job that you're too good for, and no work that won't teach you something. Working in retail, I learned the psychology of making a sale, kept a close eye on how my managers operated, and observed how HQ managed payroll and scheduling. Hostessing in restaurants was on-the-job training in thinking on my feet and interacting with customers. After high school I briefly worked reception at a commercial real estate agency. There I learned the fundamentals of working in an office, stuff like how to write a proper email and how to liaise with a client. It was basic, but I was eighteen, and I needed to learn somehow.

I did that reception job for about a year. I took it with the intention of taking a short break before going to university, but earlier that year I'd gone on a vacation to Hawaii with a girl-friend for my high school graduation trip. All the money I saved from my various jobs allowed me to travel and do things I loved at a young age, and I loved Hawaii. In fact, I liked it so much that I decided to move there instead of going back to school. Everything about Hawaii appealed to me – the laid-back vibe, the emphasis on nature, the very optimistic American attitude of everyone around me. Australians are great in a lot of ways – we are go-getters and super direct – but Americans have a borderline-delusional optimism that I found (and still find) so refreshing. Australia is small and shut off from the rest of the world, and can be really competitive as a result. We even have something called 'tall poppy syndrome', the idea being that you want to cut down anyone who is succeeding and standing out from the crowd. There's competition everywhere, of course, but in Maui there seemed to be a 'come one, come all' attitude that I wanted more of.

One of my first interactions with the US optimism I was so enamoured of came when I was a kid and moved away from my family in Australia for a few years to live in Miami, Florida, with my mother and stepfather. This also meant that I already had a US green card, which made it much easier to move to Hawaii when I wanted to – something I later realised was a huge privilege.

In many ways, making the move to Hawaii changed everything for me. In high school, my boyfriend's mom, Sonya, was a video producer, and back when her son and I were dating she hired me to help her out with wedding videography. I learned to film and edit and do production, and I loved it. While I'd worked my ass off at every job I was hired for, video production was the first one that made me think I might have found my calling. So when I moved to Maui, I got two paying jobs – one as a 'lei girl' (the girls who walk around putting flower necklaces on tourists) and another as a restaurant hostess – and I put every dollar I earned towards cameras and MacBooks and editing software. In the hope of setting up my own video production company, I started reaching out to every single hotel, fitness company, nightclub and restaurant on the island, offering to create videos for them. I did it for free initially – I'd wear my giant backpack that carried my different cameras and then edit together promotional videos they could use for marketing purposes. Basically I was making Reels before they were a thing.

At the same time as I was building my videography career, there was another life-changing development taking place. In 2009, I met Devin Brugman over Facebook and we quickly become close friends. Devin lived in LA, but she was from Maui. To this day, I can't remember exactly what we started chatting about – but it would be an understatement to say that the friendship has changed my life. We hit it off so well, and immediately became best friends, calling each other over 'Facebook-Skype' from across the world. When I left Hawaii after two years, I moved to LA and stayed with Devin in her tiny one-bedroom apartment. It was 2011, and I was a twenty-one-year-old trying to build my own video company in the film capital of the world. It was an ambitious plan, I admit, but all those years of hustling paid off. I set up my MacBook in Devin's living room and every day I sent emails to brand after brand, explaining why video was important – that it evoked an emotion you can't get from a simple photo – and trying to convince them it could enhance their marketing. Also, of course, I explained why I was *the* person they should hire to do it. Keep in mind this was before Instagram Reels or TikTok. Back then Instagram was a place where people posted their cappuccino cups with a Kelvin filter and that old-school white border. (If you know, you know!)

I ended up getting a good amount of work with swim-wear companies, and Devin would come to the shoots as my assistant. We were two young women running around with piles of equipment, trying to be professional, but each time the people running the shoots would say, 'Oh, you girls should be the one in the swimsuits! You should be in front of the camera!' (Meanwhile, we were also going to modelling agencies and trying to get signed, and we were both met with rejection left, right and centre.) We would laugh it off in an effort to be taken seriously, but the truth was that we both loved swimwear. When we weren't working, we were at the beach, baking in the sun. We wore bikinis every single day, and eventually we started posting them on Instagram. That may not sound revolutionary today, but no one was posting lifestyle shots back then. It was all scenic stuff and the afore-mentioned coffee cups.

And honestly? Some of our friends would poke fun at us for it. They thought we were crazy for posting our biki-nis and travel pictures on social media. We even had some friends who'd message us – only half-joking – saying: 'All you ever post is bikinis!' But Devin was from Maui, I was from Sydney. We grew up in swimwear, and we were young twenty-somethings living the California life. True beach girls. And I should point out that the more we posted these photos, the more followers we got. We built our personal audiences to about fifteen thousand followers, which was a lot back in those days. So one night, while we were lying around in the tiny apartment we shared, we started laughing about how some people were hating on our bikini photos, and rather than shy away from them, we decided to lean in. Screw the haters. 'You know what we should do?' I said. 'We should start a blog and just post a new bikini every single day.'

The next morning, we went to the beach, shot each other in every bikini we owned, and started a new Instagram account: A Bikini A Day. We uploaded one photo every single day, and I started reaching out to every swimwear brand I could think of, offering to 'feature' their swimsuits for $100 a post. Those hustler vibes really came in handy.

Virtually overnight, A Bikini A Day became a hit. The quality of the images was great because we had good production equipment, and there really weren't any accounts out there like it. Women were inspired by the swimwear, our friendship and our body positivity! I'll share more about how we grew the company throughout the chapters of this book – bartering services when we couldn't fund the company, building our blog, growing our audience – but over time we became pretty much the biggest online platform for swimwear in existence. We would go to Swim Week in Miami, which is the largest swimwear trade show in the world, and we were treated like total VIPs. Influencers weren't what they are today and, frankly, we were ahead of the game!

In 2013, just under two years after starting A Bikini A Day, a manufacturer we had been working with during Swim Week approached me with an idea: what if Devin and I created a swimwear line of our own? It felt like the natural next step, and after wearing nearly a thousand swimsuits between the two of us in those twenty-four months, we had a strong sense of what was missing in the market, what we liked and what we didn't. We wanted to create supportive suits to fit larger cup sizes (Devin was always frustrated that the suits we tried didn't fit her chest the way she would like), where the material felt good and looked good on camera, and made other women feel as confident in their bodies as we did.

This manufacturing company offered to partner with us – we would design the suits, it would make them and sell them exclusively through its online retailer. In the end, the partnership didn't work out. In fact, it blew up in spectacular fashion in a meeting that I'll tell you more about later, but it ended with Devin and me walking out on what until then was the biggest deal of our careers, and telling our so-called partner to shove it.

Yet out of that meeting came the business that Devin and I still run to this day. Monday Swimwear is our baby – it's an extension and offshoot of A Bikini A Day (which we eventually retired in order to build Monday), and a company that we built from nothing into a multi-million-dollar business. And everything we learned, we learned in the trenches. I didn't go to business school. I didn't even go to university. I learned by doing – sometimes that meant figuring it out as I went along, sometimes that meant asking anyone and everyone who would give me time or answers, sometimes it meant doing something the wrong way first, since every 'failure' is just an opportunity to do it right the next time. I wished there was a book that could teach me the ins and outs of launching and running and growing a business back then – all the details I needed to consider about financing and marketing and build ing an audience and pricing my products – but that book just didn't exist. Until now.

As I write this book, Monday is a ten-year-old resort fash-ion brand with a loyal customer base, a direct-to-consumer sales model and new collections launching weekly. Devin and I built the company with no outside investors – it's entirely self-funded – and today we have a team of twenty-five employees, most of whom work out of our LA office. But none of it happened overnight or by accident – Monday has been a labour of love and hustle and late nights and, yes, excessive obsession. That last bit really is the key ingredient, because as exciting as it is to run your own company it can also be exhausting and defeating and frustrating, and if you don't absolutely love what you're doing, if you're not excessively obsessed with your idea, you could easily start to hate it before it ever gets off the ground.

When I say 'excessively obsessed', I don't mean that you need to be doing something 'cool' or 'glamorous'. If you own a pest-control company, you might not be obsessed with bugs (though it doesn't hurt, and more power to you if you are), but you might be totally excited by the business model you've created, one that you believe is more efficient than that of anyone else working in that space. Or you might really believe in sustainability and green products, and the pesticides you use are what differentiate you. It's also quite likely that what you're excessively obsessed with is calling the shots and managing a big group of people and helping your clients in a way that is both lucrative for you and makes them feel a little more at ease in their clean and now pest-free space.

The point is, being excessively obsessed doesn't mean you have to be an influencer or travel to far-off places or have a job that other people covet. None of that is what makes a successful business, and I promise you it's not always as sexy as it seems. The obsession I'm talking about is when you are thinking about this company all the time – not because you're stressed and burned out and can't get a break (I don't advocate for this, and an entire section of this book is about how to maintain balance and avoid this fate) but because it energises you and gives you *that feeling.*

The truth is, entrepreneurism isn't for everyone. That's more than OK! But for some of us, it's basically in our blood. Seeped into our veins. I would start fifty companies if I could! You might be thinking, *Sure, Tash can do this, I bet she was well-off* or *She had connections,* and while I wasn't raised especially wealthy, I won't deny that I've been lucky to have certain privileges working in my favour. I had entrepreneurial parents who could give me business advice; I went to good schools as a kid; I grew up in a privileged country. Because I'd lived in Miami for a few years as a child, moving to the US in my twenties was easier than it would be for most non-US citizens. Each of these pieces contributed to a leg-up that not everyone will have, and they helped me get started as an entrepreneur. Any connection or access to capital you have in the earliest stages of building a business helps, and for me to pretend otherwise would do any reader a disservice. But privilege takes you only so far. It will help you get your business off the ground, but to stay in business, and stick with your company through the ups and downs, takes something deeper. I truly love the rush of building something from nothing and sending something you believe in out into the world. For me, that feeling of being nervous is what it is to be alive. When I don't have the excited and anxious energy that accompanies doing something I'm not totally comfortable with, that's how I know I'm not pushing myself and I need to try something new. Which is probably why, in 2020, once Monday had established itself and was getting closer and closer to being a well-oiled machine, I co-founded my next business, this time with my Pilates trainer, Jacqui Kingswell.

In March 2020, like everyone else in the world, I was on lockdown, stuck at home but wanting to stay fit and also maintain my sanity. Jacqui and I had been training in person for about a year, and at the same time that I was going stir crazy stuck inside, she was out of work due to studio shutdowns, and trying to get creative by offering classes through Instagram Live. I wasn't particularly excited to do remote Pilates – I had never really enjoyed doing virtual workouts – but it was that or nothing, so I gave it a try. And, honestly, Jacqui was incredible. Her on-screen presence was so powerful I felt like she was in the room with me. After one class, I knew we had to make the most of her talent, and I pitched her the idea of bringing her business online and taking it global. I had previously dabbled in the fitness space when I helped launch another successful fitness brand, Body by Gilles, for my ex-boyfriend (more to come later on the other companies I've helped start over the years), so I had the ideas and experience, and she had the training expertise and talent. We started The Pilates Class (TPC), an online fitness platform that offers Jacqui's unique Pilates method, combining traditional Pilates with HIIT, strength and barre classes ranging in length from five to sixty minutes. Our goal is to help our members finally find a workout they're excited to do, which makes them more inclined to be consistent and see serious results – just like I did! Whereas Monday was a product-based retail company, TPC was a service-based, digital company with a subscription model. Two very different companies and offerings and financial models, but by the end of our first year of business TPC had more than fifty thousand subscribers and millions in revenue.

Jacqui and I ended up having such a fruitful partnership that in 2023 we decided to team up on *another* business (I told you I would never stop!). When Jacqui got pregnant, she saw a huge gap in the prenatal and pregnancy category. All the birthing programmes she was doing with her husband were dull and uninspiring, but then she worked with a doula – a trained professional who served as an emotional, physical and informational guide through pregnancy and delivery – who transformed her perspective on birth and made her genuinely excited for her delivery rather than overcome by fear. Doulas can cost thousands of dollars, which of course means that, until now, only a small, privileged segment of the population could benefit from them. Jacqui and I decided to create a platform that made the doula experience accessible, so we launched The Birthing Class, an app that offers subscribers the option to choose from multiple doulas: one from the US, one from Australia and one from the UK. That way, sub-scribers can choose which doula's energy they resonate with the most and experience this unique feeling of empowerment that all women should have access to. Somehow, we ended up developing the world's first non-judgemental and user-friendly birthing-class app, with multiple doulas and birthing experts. How is it possible that this didn't already exist? Giving birth is one of the most monumental and spiritual experiences in a woman's life and in Western countries that's barely spoken of. Instead, it's treated as a medical emergency of sorts. At The Birthing Class we also have nutritionists and fitness experts on our platform, to help create a holistic and healthy birthing experience for all our users.

Now, my story is somewhat unique – I've started multiple businesses and may even launch many more. The experience comes in handy for this book, and you'll see that moments from my various companies will serve as case studies throughout these pages. But it's an unusual approach, and it's certainly not a path most entrepreneurs will aspire to ... or even one that I was aspiring to, for that matter. Starting a single business is an incredible feat, and something anyone should be seriously proud of and satisfied with. Launching a business you're passionate about, one that you can make a career of and a living wage from, and nurturing that company as it grows, is what this book is all about.

As different as all my companies are, they share at least one thing: I'm passionate about leading them in a way that feels good for me and my co-founders, respects the employees that work for us and builds a loyal customer base. And I'm not just the face of these brands, I'm in the weeds every day, looking at sales models or marketing calendars or user data or budget numbers. Almost every job at the company, I have done myself at some point. So have my co-founders. The truth is, I could talk about these companies all day – and, pretty much, I do. Just ask my husband or my dad or anyone who spends any time with me. And if you want to start your own company, that's the first requirement. My friends and followers constantly tell me they want to start businesses. Sometimes they say they have an idea they can't stop thinking about, but other times they just want to make their own schedules or get free stuff or simply escape their current day job and try something new. And while there's nothing inherently wrong with any of those reasons, at the end of the day they won't be enough if this isn't a product or service or offering that wakes you up in the night because you just can't stop thinking about it. You need to be excessively obsessed with what you do in order to survive the day-to-day struggles that your fledgling business will throw at you.

This book is for anyone considering diving into the world of entrepreneurship, no matter what your business idea. You don't need to be in a 'glamorous' field to get something out of these pages – they're for anyone who believes in what they want to build. I'll share everything I've learned since those early days at A Bikini A Day, from what you need to think about before you even begin, to how to keep your company running smoothly when you're growing at a rapid rate. It's a practical and how-to business guide for the new world, where customer bases are built on Instagram or TikTok, and all the glamour of #hustleculture is showcased online yet the many risks are still kept largely hush-hush. I'll offer advice on executing a successful business, building it from nothing (this book isn't about raising capital, although if that's your goal there's still plenty to learn here) and marketing your offering in today's digital world. We'll cover the ins and outs of generating a huge brand following, including how to come up with your company name, when to take a salary, how to be a good manager and the psychology of marketing. We'll discuss how to take a calculated risk, how to stay true to your core brand values and how to pick yourself up again in the face of the inevitable setbacks. And I'll reveal how I got it done each step of the way, and what I've learned works – and what absolutely doesn't.

Once you're sufficiently inspired to get out there and hustle, we'll focus on the most important piece of all: how to take care of yourself and slow down when your career adrenaline is telling you to pick up the pace. Because, I promise, nothing will take your business out faster than a burned-out leader who can no longer steer the ship. Working around the clock with no breaks or balance is not a recipe for longevity. Just the opposite. It can be detrimental to your physical and mental health, and your business should be a point of pride and joy, not a source of misery or strain. If you are truly excessively obsessed, perhaps the hardest thing I will ask of you in this whole book is to slow down, breathe and take a moment for yourself. It is also the most important.

When you close this book, you'll either feel excited and ready to take a leap of faith, or exhausted and turned off at the mere thought of being a CEO or business owner. Both

feelings are completely valid! In fact, they're equally important to pay attention to, because running a business is not for
everyone. There is absolutely nothing wrong with realising
that your purpose is actually to be a great team player, give
your all to your role and clock out at the end of the day. Hell,
I would be nowhere without the teams that work on Monday
and TPC. But no matter who you are, my hope is that you
will learn something in this book about work, passion and
the importance of being intentional about your career. I hope
you'll take away something that you can apply to whatever
it is that you're passionate about, whether that's today or ten
years from now.

The truth is, my life's purpose is not to get the world to
wear bathing suits or take Pilates classes. It's to help people
feel confident. And nothing will make you feel more confident
than pursuing a passion that is truly your calling, and doing
so armed with more knowledge and less fear. So let's get
started – your career is waiting.

PART 1

Before we begin

1

What's the big idea?

There's no shortage of remarkable ideas, what's missing is the will to execute them.

SETH GODIN

Building a company is a labour of love. And there's a lot you have to love: your business idea, hopefully, but also being a leader and making decisions, and ultimately being responsible for the success, or failure, of whatever your venture. It's not quite that simple, of course. No single person can take the credit for a company's success, and no one is entirely responsible if it goes under, but if you are the owner and CEO of a small business, the business's future ultimately falls to you. It might sound flippant to say you need to feel excessively obsessed, but it's the truth, because on top of the sheer workload necessary to get a business up and running, if you're not passionate about your mission and your offering how can you expect your staff or your customers to be?

Before even starting A Bikini A Day, I lived and breathed swimwear. I grew up in Sydney and Miami, spent two years in Maui, and then moved to LA – beach culture was a part of my very being. But it wasn't just that I *wore* a lot of bathing suits, I *knew* them. I knew which fabrics looked luxurious and which looked cheap. Which styles flattered and which dug in and made a woman feel uncomfortable. And yet, when I woke up in the middle of the night to jot down notes about how we could grow, or new content we could create, it wasn't because of how much I adored swimsuits. It was because I felt confident that I understood this demographic of women who were just like Devin and me – beach girls who never really cared about bags or shoes but who coveted bikinis – better than anyone else. I knew what they were interested in, what turned them off, what they were inspired by. I knew that the calibre of our content, in terms of high-quality photography and beautiful locations, would resonate more than catalogue-type shots, and that if our followers were going to engage with more content from us, they'd want to see similar luxe beach beauty and fitness and travel content. Armed with all that knowledge, I was also entirely sure that I was on to something, and that with enough hard work I could turn this idea into something huge.

That feeling – the inkling of 'holy shit this could be big' that reverberated through my whole body – is what woke me up in the middle of night. I didn't want to miss this opportunity that I could so clearly see the potential in. There was also the slight satisfaction of proving all the naysayers wrong. Despite all those haters who said 'stop posting in bikinis', here we were, wearing bikinis all day every day and getting paid for it! At one point I spoke to a family friend, a very successful businessman, about A Bikini A Day and the ways in which we planned to grow it into a profitable endeavour, and his response was: 'Respectfully, I think your time would be better spent in college.'

Plus, there was the rush I got from building something

out of nothing – here was an idea Devin and I had come up with, all on our own, and we were creating a major career for ourselves (and one we absolutely loved) thanks mostly to our work ethic and the sheer amount of time and energy we'd put into working a million jobs and learning to hustle.

Here for the wrong reasons

I spend a lot, and I mean a lot, of time talking to people who want to be entrepreneurs and giving them advice. During these conversations, one of the first questions I ask is 'Why do you want to do this?' I'll tell you, there are some very common answers that are clear signs entrepreneurism isn't the right path forward ...

Reason 1: 'I hate my job'

There are a lot of questions to ask yourself if you hate your job. Is it the line of work you're in? Do you actually like the work you do, but your company treats its employees like shit and morale is in the toilet? Are you simply bored and need a new challenge? Do you want a pay rise or a promotion? Feeling undervalued and underpaid are good reasons to leave the job you're in, but they don't necessarily warrant starting your own business. Maybe what you really need is to find a different company that sees your true value, or to make yourself irreplaceable at your current workplace so you have more bargaining power. You don't want to be running *away* from something, you want to be running *towards* ... towards your passion or towards financial independence or towards other specific goals you have set for yourself.

Also, if you're just trying to escape having to answer to

someone or getting a shitty pay cheque ... well, first of all, there's always someone to answer to. If you take on investors, they will have constant questions about business performance and strategy decisions, and you will always have to report in to them. I purposely haven't taken on investors in either of my companies – between my influencer earnings and a couple of small personal loans (and some cost-saving decisions I'll tell you about soon) I was able to fund Monday myself. I didn't want the additional oversight of investors or a board. But I have a business partner and, most importantly, I have customers. Today's customers hold business owners more accountable than ever. That's a good thing, really, but this idea that you can quit your job and launch a business and do whatever you want, unchecked, is a myth. And we'll get into the nitty-gritty of finances shortly, but the idea that you're going to get a bigger and better pay cheque from your fledgling small business is very likely to be misguided. The truth is that you probably won't make real money or take home a good salary for a while. When Devin and I started Monday, every dollar we made went back into the business, and that was true for a few years.

Reason 2: 'Being an entrepreneur looks so glamorous'

There's another variation of this answer I hear a lot too, which is something along the lines of 'I want what you have – to be able to do whatever I want and buy whatever I want.' I'm guessing you already know, deep down, that there's more to running a business than what you see on social media or read about in articles. Entrepreneurs rarely share the boring parts – the meetings and the days spent poring over spreadsheets – because who wants to look at that? What you're seeing in people's social media feeds are the very best, most fabulous moments because it's part of that business owner's branding and marketing strategy. But it's also because if you are a good leader, you want to be inspirational and positive. You don't want to focus on the negative. Not to mention the fact that I don't have time to document it all – I'm too busy working.

And, listen, I'm not going to deny that my life, particularly owning a swimwear company and being an influencer, is a real dream sometimes – I *do* travel to stunning locations and work with incredible people – however, not only did I work really hard for it but also a lot of people would truly hate it. I travelled nine months of the year and was away from my family and friends for eight years in a row. Devin and I would go on month-long trips and by the end we'd be so sick of taking photos of ourselves that we could have given up right then and there. And this is not a 'poor me' moment, because I love what I do and feel so lucky to do it, but for anyone in business – hell, for anyone in the world – what you see on social is not the whole story, and if you start your business expecting all of that and none of the exceedingly unglamorous but necessary work of, say, securing URLs or filing business paperwork or looking at sales data, then you'll be sorely disappointed, and probably over your job before it ever really starts.

Reason 3: 'I feel like I'm meant for something more'

OK, sure, that might be true ... but *what* are you meant for? Putting your intention into the universe is great, but it needs to be aligned with introspection. You need to have a concept you can actually explain, and that you believe in. 'I know there's more out there' is a pretty easy thing to say when you're feeling uninspired at your job, but there needs to be some action behind it. What is your passion? I mean, of course there's more out there – there's a whole word of stuff that isn't your particular day job – but that doesn't mean it's meant for you. If you want to be an entrepreneur because you feel called to it, consider that a whisper. It's a first step. Next you have to figure out what you actually want to do and how you will turn what you do into a business. Or, don't! Maybe the 'more' you're meant for is to take up a hobby, or to carve out more time for your family. Not everything needs to be a business, so now's the time to lock into *your* particular purpose. It won't be the same for everyone.

Reason 4: 'I want more freedom'

I guess it depends here how you define freedom. If you mean you want to be your own boss then, yes, that will happen. But if you mean you want more time for yourself, to be with friends or watch TV or take a bath ... well, you know already what I'm going to say. Starting a business is like running on a hamster wheel, and the time off is minimal, maybe even non-existent. Luckily, that old cliché is true, that when you love what you do you don't feel like you've worked a day in your life, but it will take time away from a lot of the things you love, like family and friends and hobbies and sleep. You might do it and realise that, to you, freedom is being able to clock in and clock out, and then have your evenings and weekends offline. I am never offline. No matter what time of day it is, I am literally always available. It's a choice, but it's not everyone's version of freedom.

Finally, if you hire employees, then you have people whose livelihoods depend on you, which is a massive responsibility. Starting a business does not feel like a huge weight has been lifted off your shoulders – in fact, it can feel more like the weight of the world if you don't go in with a clear plan and passion, and if you don't get real fulfilment out of running the show.

There are other reasons for starting a business, of course, and I hear those too. Maybe there's a service someone really needs that doesn't exist, so they want to create it. Maybe they've learned a lot in their field of work – so much so that they have an idea that could disrupt the market, and they want to create a company around that. Maybe there's a product they make at home that everyone in their life adores and they think they can sell it. What I tell people in all of these conversations is to start with some reasonable goal: I want to make X amount of money and be my own boss and love what I do and be happy. That alone is a pretty great life. Everything else after that is a bonus.

It's not for everyone

I absolutely love what I do. I wouldn't want to do anything different. Despite all the hours I put into my different jobs as a teenager, I seriously couldn't imagine myself working for a company that wasn't mine and I wasn't wholly invested in. Owning your own business is thrilling, rewarding and emotional; it makes you feel half dead and at the same time more alive than you've ever felt. But ultimately you need to be prepared to sacrifice a lot to maybe, just maybe, make it big and be rich – but more likely to experience something that pushes you out of your comfort zone and puts you in your purpose.

Having said all that, I don't want to talk anyone out of pursuing their dream. If you have an idea that you can't shake and you want to give it a go, or you're curious if your nugget of an idea has the potential for something bigger, this is the book for you. There's so much opportunity out there, and you've already taken the first step by choosing to learn more! I hope to provide actionable advice so that you can read in these pages all the lessons I've learned the hard way over the last decade. I hope it saves you time and allows you to pursue your passion without all the hiccups (though there will always be hiccups, that's just part of the adventure). And, frankly, the world needs more passionate and purpose-driven business owners. But if reading about the workload and the sacrifice makes you want to take to your bed, then entrepreneurism may not be for you, and that's OK too. In fact, it's a really good thing to know. Social media and hustle culture glorify being a boss and a business owner, but it is just as noble to be a person who works Monday to Friday, nine to five, and simply does good work at the job they've been hired for. Our world needs to do a better job of celebrating both paths equally.

Understanding your business idea

Now let's get down to, well, business. Before you can actually *start* anything, it's critical to get really clear on what you are creating and offering. This book is generally about running a small business, so I'm not focusing on how to build a media empire or a logistics company (which, if you're not sure what that means, might be a shipping company or a warehouse). The small business you create might grow and scale and no longer qualify as 'small' – that may or may not be your goal – but these lessons will continue to come in handy.

The first thing you need to ask yourself is, what industry,

at a high level, do you want to be in? Goods or services? Once you know that, it's time to get even more granular. Is it a physical product, like clothing or jewellery or stationery? Or is it an online service, like a ride-share or fitness or a community platform? You might also be thinking about an in-person service, like the pest-control company, or a physical service space like a restaurant or spa. My experience is largely in selling a physical product online (Monday Swimwear) and an online service (The Pilates Class), so I'll focus mostly on those two, though if your dream is to, say, open a restaurant, these lessons are largely transferable.

There are pros and cons to every business structure. Or, if they aren't cons necessarily, they are definitely additional considerations that can be tricky to navigate. One is not better or smarter or more lucrative than another, but there are definitely factors to consider that are specific to each category, and it's best to know that going in. The lists below are certainly not exhaustive, and each individual business will have its own considerations based on what you're selling, but here are some initial elements to keep in mind as you begin to think through your idea ...

Product-based business

I'll admit, all else being equal, I really love having a physical product. Interacting with it and, in my case, wearing it – there's a real rush to holding something in your hand that you created. To see it come to life is just so amazing.

Product pros

- You can hold it in your hand! The physicality of having a product that you can engage with is really special – there's nothing like looking at a physical item that was conceived entirely in your head.

- If you are launching new styles of your product regularly, you consistently have something new to talk about and to get your customer excited for, which makes marketing a lot easier.
- Showcasing your product to the customer is easy. First of all, everyone knows what a swimsuit or a jacket or a table is; you don't have to explain how it works or what it docs. But cvcn if you're selling a high-end coffee maker that does necessitate describing the different fancy things it does, this is an item you can photograph and show on your website, or post a video of someone using.
- Pricing is easier, because people are more willing to pay for things they can touch or feel. Just think about it: you are probably totally willing to spend $60 on a new pair of yoga pants, but you might hesitate to spend $4 a month on an app.
- If you can create an amazing product and build a loyal customer base, you can build a very steady, reliable business. You do one specific thing, and do it well.

Drawbacks and potential challenges

- There are a lot of logistics to sort through in terms of creating and storing the physical product. Will you be doing that in your home when you first start out? Or will you get a storage facility? Will you do it yourself or hire a team? Do you need a manufacturer?
- Supply chain issues are real. Since we have a manufacturer who makes our Monday suits and sends them to us, we're susceptible to any issues that arise

along the way – if we don't have a product then we can't sell a product. A shipping container might go missing, and that's entirely out of our control, but it can still screw things up pretty royally. At Monday we once had an entire shipment of suits where the dye was running, so we couldn't sell any of them and had no money coming in for months.

- Overheads are high. You're likely to need a large upfront investment in order to create the product itself, and you'll need it long before you have anything to sell.
- Redundant inventory. This is any inventory that you don't need any more, maybe because it didn't sell or because you've updated your product. At A Bikini A Day we once created swimsuit calendars, and we ordered five thousand but only sold two thousand. That was a (relatively) cheap lesson for us in avoiding redundant inventory and not over-ordering. And this isn't just an issue of losing money. Redundant inventory can contribute to wastefulness in your industry, so figuring out how to purchase generally accurate quantities and then properly 'dispose' of any leftover stock can be its own mess. (This is one of the reasons some new industries, like fast fashion, are so despised – they order huge amounts of inventory, which most of the time is not manufactured ethically, to keep up with demand, and this results in them being extremely wasteful. This allows them to grow but throws any environmental or social responsibility out the window.) At Monday, we place our inventory orders to sell out and only have sales twice a year. We believe in manufacturing a premium product and ordering only what we need to avoid adding wasteful stock to the world.

- Growth goes at a slower pace. Since you now know
  that you want to be smart about not over-ordering
  your product, you need to scale in a thoughtful way.
  If the demand is high, fulfilment can take time. Each
  product needs to get made, and, when you have smaller
  quantities of product as well as fewer employees,
  supply doesn't always match demand.
- Returns. You can't sell a physical product without
  deciding how you will handle returns. For example,
  some of the garments that are returned to Monday
  need to be dry cleaned, and all returned products need
  to be repackaged so that they're as good as new for
  the next customer. That won't be the case, specifically,
  if you're not selling clothing, but in this day and age,
  people expect to be able to return what they buy, so
  you need to account for that.
- Shipping. If you're selling your product in a retail store
  this won't be as much of an issue, but since Monday
  is online and direct to consumer (as are an increasing
  number of businesses), we have costs associated with
  that, and the reality is that shipping costs are at an
  all-time high and only going up. If you have, say, a
  candle company, that's an important thing to consider,
  because candles are heavy and cost a lot to ship.

Service-based businesses

Service pros

- You can capitalise on your expertise. The Pilates
  Class came into being because Jacqui is an incredible

instructor – we didn't need to create something out
of nothing, because she was already offering the
exact same product but on a smaller scale. Service
businesses largely rely on people who are already
experts in their field, whether we're talking about a
masseuse or an exterminator or anything in between.

- Overhead costs are low. If you don't need to create
  inventory or ship goods, you'll have far fewer costs
  associated with selling your product once you're up
  and running, and nothing to get rid of if you don't
  'sell out'.
- If people love what you offer, you can grow at a rapid
  rate. The ability to serve your customers doesn't rely
  on the supply chain or the production and shipping
  of goods, which means you can scale exponentially
  faster and literally grow while you sleep.
- If it's an online service, you can go global. Shipping a
  swimsuit internationally is pricey, which is why you
  might see companies that can't or won't ship out of
  their own country or to certain areas. Going online
  is the great equaliser – at The Pilates Class, we have
  users in more than 120 countries.
- The rapid development of easy-to-learn online
  platforms and tools like Shopify, Vimeo, Mailchimp
  and more (see the full list of my most-used tools
  on page 132) means you can start an online service
  company all by yourself. You don't need to rely on
  someone else to, say, sew up a swimsuit for you.
- If you do well online, with low overhead costs and
  a high profit, you create the potential to fund new
  revenue streams for your company that require
  investments you may not have had initially. After the
  initial success of TPC online, we were able to open

pop-up studios so that some customers could have a more tactile experience with our brand.

Drawbacks and potential challenges

- Educating your consumer about what it is you *do*, exactly, can be hard. Think of something like Uber – when it first started, a lot of effort went into explaining the concept because ride-shares were new and different and, for some users, totally confusing. People generally underestimate how difficult it is to explain what your business is in only a few words, and with a service you don't have something you can photograph or show off to help with that understanding. As a result, you might need to pay relatively high marketing costs.
- If you are launching a tailored online service that needs brand new or very specific features, you'll need to spend quite a bit upfront to launch the app or website.
- Pricing can be tricky. As I mentioned earlier, if people don't have something that appeals to one of their five senses it can be a harder sell. I'll get into the psychology of pricing on page 126, but convincing consumers to spend when they won't get something physical in return can be an uphill battle.
- Over time, your service might expand in reach or range, but you're less likely to add new products to your line because, well, you don't have a product. And yet, in every business, you need to constantly think of new ways to promote or attract new customers. When you don't have an exciting new launch you can capitalise on, it can feel like you need to constantly reinvent your marketing or promotional efforts in order to grow your client base.

- If your company relies on tech to provide its service or book appointments, then you'd better hope your servers stay up and running! Even the biggest companies in the world can get hacked, or sites go down or load slowly, and that's a really quick way to lose customers. There's a constant pressure to have good coders and good platforms. And if that tech is your one and only way to connect with your customer, you essentially have all your eggs in one basket.

- If your service is entirely online, like Uber or The Pilates Class (although we do now have some pop-up studios, as noted above, it's still an online service business), then the rat race to create new features or update old ones is pretty much never ending. Tech moves so fast: by the time you are ready to launch your first iteration, competing companies may have already launched a new feature that will take ten months to build – it can already feel like you're a year behind.

None of the aforementioned pros are explicit reasons to go into a specific business, and none of the drawbacks are reasons to necessarily stay away. Restaurants, for example, are incredibly hard businesses to maintain – the overhead costs are extremely high and you might be working seven days a week – but, if food is your passion, I'll always say you should do it. You may not have the potential to make as much money or grow as quickly as you would with a scalable online business, but it will still be more successful than if you're running a company you don't care about. You should absolutely do the thing you're obsessed with, because that's what will sustain you when you are working instead of, say, spending time with your family. I just want you to be completely clear on what awaits you when you decide to dive in. The more you know ahead of time, the fewer surprises await you on the other side.

Think about the long term

One final note about figuring out your business idea: remember, if all goes well, this business will be in your life for a long time. I hear so often about people who start a business and they're so excited to launch they don't think very much about what it might look like five, ten, even twenty, years down the line. But once you launch a company, it's part of your life, potentially for ever. Maybe you'll sell it one day, or maybe it will fold, but it's always a part of your story, and hopefully a great part. Still, I've had moments after starting my companies where I've thought, *Shit, I'm in this for the long haul.* If you're not sure how you feel about something, don't launch and assume you'll figure out if you like it later. Dip your toe in – maybe work for someone else in the same industry – before you fully commit. Hopefully you'll learn for certain what you thought you knew all along: that this is what you were made for, and there's no one better suited to building your business than you.

2

How do you afford it?

Quitting your full-time job to start a company is like proposing marriage on the first date ... Don't go in all guns blazing. Start it as a hobby and see if it takes off.

ADAM GRANT

Funding the business is one of the biggest and most critical hurdles for start-ups. It takes money to make money, as they say, and it's true: you can't start a business without a reserve of cash. There's certainly a lot you can do to keep costs down, and I'll get into those tricks of the trade shortly, but no matter how cost-conscious you are, you'll need *some* financing to get products made or to build out your service or to ship purchases and hire employees. Securing funding is especially difficult for women. Women-led start-ups receive less than 3 per cent of all venture capitalist (VC) investments, according to data from PitchBook, a website devoted to research on global capital markets. That number has to change, but it's taking longer than it should, and I am here to make sure you go into business with your eyes wide open and an understanding of the challenges you might face.

In some ways, money is an important barrier to entry and serves a purpose. If we all had unlimited funding I can't imagine how many unnecessary or redundant or wasteful businesses would pop up. That said, it's really a shame to think of how many great and life-changing ideas go unexplored due to this major hurdle. There's a saying that you should never use your own money to fund your business, and there are some truths to it because using your own money can be risky and leave you in a tough spot if things don't go according to plan. Most aspiring business owners I know take the pitch-the-VC-firms-and-raise-the-money route for that very reason. I'm not covering that process in this book because (a) I've never done it and (b) I think it should be your last resort. Giving away a percentage of your business to someone who, in most cases, you barely know and then signing up to work with them indefinitely is a huge risk in itself. The partnership could be a bad fit, or they could steer you away from your true vision for the business. My hope is that with the tips I'm providing in this book, you will protect yourself from some of the riskier elements of self-funding. Still, when you have no other options or the idea you're obsessed with really needs a large amount of capital to get up and running, then raising money is definitely one of your options and you should absolutely consider it ... just proceed with caution.

The big question: 'Should I quit my job?'

Nearly every time I've started a company, I have worked at least one other job at the same time. While I was trying to launch my videography business in Hawaii, I was working as a lei girl and restaurant hostess. By the time we started A Bikini A Day, I had transitioned my videography work to Los

Angeles and was living off that income. When we launched Monday, I was making a full-time living as an influencer and brand ambassador, and still bringing in money at A Bikini A Day. It's thrilling and a major adrenaline rush to launch a new business, but excitement doesn't pay the bills, so, at least in the beginning, it's important to be realistic about how you're going to support yourself *and* your fledgling company as you work to get it off the ground.

When you first start a new venture, every dollar counts. Businesses require money for a successful launch, and I've never taken on financing or raised capital, which means my business partners and I have always funded our own projects. I prefer this model for a number of reasons, all of which I'll cover more in the next part of this book, but the short version is that I don't want to give up ownership or have to answer to a bunch of investors unless it's absolutely necessary. Still, that means it's my responsibility to figure out how to cover all the start-up costs. And on top of that, especially in my earliest days of entrepreneurship, it meant I had to figure out how to live! Some people get financial support from a parent or a partner while they try to build their business, which is a fantastic option if you have it, but it wasn't my situation. I needed to cover rent and groceries and all my living expenses, and the only way to do that was by having a second (and sometimes a third) job. And as tiring and busy and chaotic as that felt, it's what I would recommend to anyone and everyone who's considering launching their own business. First of all, it's a safety net. Think of yourself as a business – you always want multiple revenue streams. Second, working for someone else will give you an inside peek at how other companies do business. On top of that, the working-multiple-jobs hustle will give you an immense appreciation for the small wins that happen as you work towards the big ones.

In the earliest days of A Bikini A Day, Devin and I were living in a tiny two-bedroom apartment in the Brentwood neighbourhood of Los Angeles. Our rent was $1,600 a month – or $800 each – and every month I was scrambling. I was getting videography work, but it was always *just enough* to get by. Every month I was looking at my finances and thinking, *How am I going to pay rent?* And yet, the days I spent in the Brentwood apartment are some of the best memories of my life. Every little win felt so hard earned, and because of that we appreciated them *so much*. I will never forget the day Devin and I bought a new fridge. We had worked so, so hard for the money to cover it, so it was the biggest deal in the world to us when that delivery truck rolled up. It wasn't a fancy fridge or anything. But it was new, and it was ours, and it was purchased with the money we earned ourselves, from a business we created. We were so freaking excited.

As your business grows and you find more success, it gets easier to overlook the little things. You're so focused on the major milestones that you forget to appreciate the minor blessings and wins along the way. But business ownership is such a roller coaster that if you don't appreciate the small victories, it's far easier to burn out. (To this day, my online bios all read, 'Appreciate the little things & the big things will come', and I believe that wholeheartedly, because I've lived it.) When you're working multiple jobs and trying to figure out how you're going to pay for groceries and your company's new website all at the same time, each small step in the right direction feels like a major leap. That's an attitude you want to cultivate early and hold on to as long as you can – and it's a lot easier to appreciate something when you've worked your ass off for it.

Killing the game when you don't want to play

When you've got a business idea that you're super excited about, it's normal to want to get started this very second. Why would you waste your time on a job you don't love – or, worse, a job you actively hate – when you've identified your calling and want to focus on that?

As I've said, there's real life to consider. Things like rent or car payments or electricity bills, all of which require actual money. Quitting your paying job to focus on your business before any cash comes in is probably not a sustainable solution for most people, and it's also not a great choice for your business – an entrepreneur who can barely support herself has a much shorter runway in terms of how long she can dedicate to building something from nothing. Also, research shows that business owners who engage in 'hybrid entrepreneurship' – meaning they start their business while still working their day job – are 33 per cent less likely to fail in their new endeavour. This book is about creating a business that will last, so rather than jumping in head first, the question is, how can you wade in gradually, so that by the time you're fully submerged, you're comfortable and in control? It's going to start, for better or worse, with collecting an income elsewhere.

When Devin and I started Monday, we didn't take a salary from the company for four years. We didn't necessarily *have* to wait that long, and you may not either, but at that point we were both living off the income we made as influencers. I still do influencer work and it's work that I enjoy – I especially love how creative I get to be, and how supportive my followers are and always have been – but I'm not passionate enough about it to make it my main focus. It helped fund Monday and was a great platform on which to build brand recognition (more on this later), but my true love has always been the work I've done behind the scenes. If I had to choose between influencing and running a business, I'd choose the business every time. Still, it paid the bills without taking too much time away from my main focus, which was Monday. If your business takes off, it may not be possible for you to forgo a salary for that long even if you want to, because you may not have the bandwidth to work two full-time jobs. But the longer you can go without taking a salary, the more money you will be able to reinvest into the company to facilitate growth (again, more on this soon).

If you approach the work you *must* do to earn a living in the right way, you can make the job work for you just as hard as you're working for the job. Your heart may be entirely in your passion project, but while you're taking home a pay cheque from someone else, you can use your access within that company to gather information that will help you down the road. In addition to helping finance your lifestyle, collecting an income from a second job means you'll have an opportunity to observe the many aspects of running a company that you probably never even contemplated when you came up with your big idea. If you want to start a business selling beautifully designed hats, for example, you probably haven't spent much time considering how you'll handle payroll or HR or taxes or hiring and firing. You've just thought about the hats! What they'll look like, why people will love them, maybe the many different styles you will make and where you'll get the materials. But when it comes to starting a business it *all* matters. In fact, according to a January 2011 article in *Entrepreneur* magazine, entrepreneurs spend about 40 per cent of their time on tasks that don't directly generate income – if those duties, like payroll or HR or accounting or hiring, are completely ill-conceived or handled by someone who doesn't know what they're doing, the company could go under even if the hats are totally gorgeous.

I worked a zillion different jobs before I started A Bikini A Day, and while I absolutely wanted to be the best at all of them, I certainly did not love all of them. In fact, plenty of them I hated – especially those retail jobs where I was forced to be on my feet, in high heels, all day. But I've always believed that if I'm going to spend my time doing something, I'm going to learn from it. In school I didn't gravitate towards maths or science, so when I had bosses who made me cash up the register at the end of the day or dig into Excel spreadsheets filled with columns of numbers, my eyes would begin to glaze over. But I forced myself to wake up and get it right because it was my job and, as it turned out, when I started my own company every one of those pieces came into play.

I know so many people who are unhappy in their jobs, and they go to the office every day thinking *This job isn't for me*, spending their hours from nine to five daydreaming about what else is out there. But if you're working in a business, even if you can't stand the job, you are *inside* the business, so pay attention. I promise, it's so much easier to deconstruct how and why a company works when you have access – looking at a business from the outside will never give you the full picture. So start taking notes. What different departments does it have? What does each department do? Meet people, ask questions, show interest. If you are kind and respectful and show a genuine curiosity about what someone does or why they do it, people are very forthcoming with information. More often than not they will be happy to teach you or show you the ropes. And most of what one company does, yours will have to do too. No matter what product you sell or service you offer, all companies need to hire and pay employees. They need to calculate profit margins and deal with customer or client feedback and navigate legal contracts and market their offerings, so you never know when the stuff you're learning will come in handy.

And when I say pay attention, please remember that no detail is too small. You might be assigned some extremely mundane tasks, but no matter how seemingly stupid or insignificant or irrelevant they seem, those same details are likely to come up again when your business is live. In summer 2023, we opened our first Monday pop-up shop at The Grove, a high-end outdoor mall in Los Angeles. As we considered various customer service and experience details that we wanted to implement, I couldn't help thinking about my time working the retail floor and I implemented a lot of what I knew from back then. When I was a teenager putting out clothing displays at the mall, did I think I was learning anything that would be useful to me one day? Not really. But there I was twenty years later, remembering what looked good back then and how customers interacted with it.

So instead of simply resigning yourself to the fact that you may have to work two jobs for a bit, I encourage you to look at your paying gig not as a detour on your path but as an integral part of the journey. Do your job as best as you can, even if it's not your calling. I'm a big believer that when you commit yourself to whatever you're doing, accept that it's where you are in that moment, and work as hard as you can to excel in that space: the universe will open up for you. It might sound a little woo-woo, but I've seen it too many times to ignore it. The moment you accept your situation rather than fight it, *that's* when the next exciting opportunity comes along. Even if it doesn't seem like you're on the right path, if you're putting in the work rather than just putting in the hours, you are progressing.

The freedom of working a second job

Here's a truth of entrepreneurship that will probably sound counter-intuitive: working a second job will create significant freedom in the early stages of your business.

I know, the idea of working for someone else when your professional dream is to work for yourself may sound a lot more like handcuffs than freedom. I get that. But when you first start a company, there is nothing more important than trying new things and taking risks and finding out what works and what doesn't. That's really hard to do when your livelihood entirely depends on every dollar your new business brings in. After all, a lot of the risks you're going to take and new approaches you're going to try – stuff like product launches or marketing campaigns or outside vendors you want to hire – cost money. If the only money you have to live off is the cash coming in from your business, experimenting with new (and, yes, sometimes costly) ideas can feel irresponsible.

At Monday, because Devin and I didn't take a salary for so long, all the money we made from the business went back into the business. When we wanted to try something different or had a new idea, we never wondered, *Hmm, should we spend money on that? If we do, we might not take home as much*, because, frankly, we weren't taking home anything. We thought of it as Monday's money, not *our* money, so as far as we were concerned, all that spending was literally the cost of doing business. Had we taken money out, we might have been more hesitant to try new things and experiment. After all, if the money from your start-up venture is the only money you are making, you're more likely to overanalyse risk, which can slow you down. You might be scared to do anything that could potentially decrease your income. Especially in the earliest days of business, I believe in throwing ideas at the wall to see what sticks. I'm all about picking up the pace and riding the wave of momentum.

To be clear, a desire to preserve your income and bring home more money is human nature – it has nothing to do with greed – but introducing a fear of risk can negatively affect a business. It takes away from the trial and error and the willingness to fail, and that experimental attitude is critical to a company's ability to find its footing, especially in the early days. A fear of spending will hold you back and stifle innovation. When you have a second job with a steady pay cheque, you aren't risking your living wage. You are free to be creative and try new things. When your ability to pay the rent is directly tied to how much your business makes, you'll be less focused on the potential opportunities created by innovation and far more fixated on everything that could go wrong.

I don't want to overlook the fact that working two jobs is tough. When you have a job that requires you to work full-time (or more!), putting in the off-hours work to launch a business is a big undertaking. I get it! If working two jobs feels completely unrealistic, perhaps you can downshift your employment to part-time so that you can keep a partial pay cheque while you get your business off the ground. You might also have kids to raise, or maybe you're thinking about starting a family, and doing that plus a job *plus* starting a business is a lot. I always say my businesses are my babies, because they seem to require the same amount of love and attention. The point is, I'm not minimising how much work this all takes, and everyone's situation will be different, but I know two things for sure: nothing lasts for ever, this period of hustle included; and if anyone can do it all, it's women! I grew up watching my mom juggle business and family, and I'm still inspired by her. If you are the kind of person who wants to run a company, then I'm confident you already have it in you.

Exceptions to the rule

There will be times when working a day job while starting your business doesn't make sense, or simply isn't the right thing to do, even if you need the stability. If, for example, your entrepreneurship work presents a conflict of interest with your ability to perform at your job, you will have to make a choice. You certainly don't want to start out in the business world doing anything sneaky or shady (even if you don't realise you are doing so) – industries are small and connections are critical, so you don't want to burn any bridges or do anything unethical. You may also want to check your employment contract or company policies, or even just have a sit-down with your boss, to be clear on what's acceptable.

If you decide to bring in investors to fund your company, you may find that they aren't thrilled about you splitting your time. If their money is wrapped up in your business, it's not unreasonable for them to hope you will give it your undivided attention (in that case, maybe part of your funding includes raising the money to pay yourself an income so you can dedicate 100 per cent of your time to the business). You may find you have to make some hard decisions about what the right path forward for you and your career is, but consider it practice. Being a business owner is all about making hard decisions, so exercising that muscle will only help you in the long run.

The barter system

Since my videography work earned me just enough money to pay my bills while launching A Bikini A Day, it certainly didn't bring in any extra cash to invest in the business. We didn't have a ton of early expenses – no employees to pay, no office space to rent, no products to ship – but all businesses have start-up costs, and many of them we couldn't afford. Although I had no money to offer, I did have skills, and trading goods and services became an early lifeline for our brand.

It started with our website. We wanted something that looked better than a DIY blog, and a friend of mine had a father who was a web designer. He wasn't some fancy tech guy, but he knew how to code and could create a decent-looking web page. He was also building a company of his own, making sustainable clothing, so I told him that I would shoot his launch campaign if he would build us a website. Considering the fact that, today, a custom-designed website can cost upwards of $10,000, bartering can be a really smart cost-saver when you're just starting out. I was constantly trading my talents in photography or videography for the services that our business sorely needed but couldn't afford.

When I say that you need to hustle to get your business off the ground, this is what I'm talking about. Figuring out how to get shit done even when you have limited resources. You need to be inventive around securing your business needs so as not to throw money at unnecessary costs. Do you have a friend who is an accountant? Do you know how to create engaging social media posts? Great! You can help each other out by exchanging these services without ever spending a penny. Trading your talents to get things cheaper, or even free, is an oft-overlooked option for those who are new to the business world. You fixate so much on costs and overhead expenses that you forget that money is not the only thing of value. But in today's business world the barter economy is growing quite fast. According to 2023 information from the International Reciprocal Trade Association website, about $12–14 billion a year is exchanged worldwide in barter or trade transactions, and that number is only growing, which means you are definitely not the only person looking to make a deal.

As you think about what type of trades could make sense to keep monetary costs down, consider both goods and services. If you make a physical product and have extra inventory, you could certainly use the product as a form of currency. If, like The Pilates Class, you have an online service, it will be a low cost to the business to give someone a free subscription in exchange for their services or collaborate to promote them on your platform in some way. But in the earliest stages, when you are just trying to get your business up and running, you may not even have the product or service to offer yet. And of course a trade only works if both sides are getting something out of it that they need and value. This is why bartering services is often a better approach – no matter what your company does, there are certain services that all businesses need.

What skills can you barter?

As you think about what you need in order to start your business, take stock of your own skills and talents. What can you do that might be valuable to another person's company? The list below covers a lot of common services that all businesses need, and I hope it will help you pinpoint the skills you already have that you can use to your benefit. But, remember, this list is by no means exhaustive. Maybe you're a great public speaker and can help someone get ready to pitch investors or give an interview. Or you're a personal trainer and can offer fitness classes to small groups of employees. Or maybe you have an apartment that your friend can work out of – now you're offering her office space, what can she offer you in return? So much of launching a business is about being creative and thinking outside the box, so start now!

Skills you can barter

These might include:

- social media marketing
- copywriting/copy-editing
- website building/search engine optimisation
- accounting/bookkeeping
- photography/videography
- contract review/legal
- data analysis
- graphic design
- creative consultancy
- event planning

Forgo the glamour, call in the favours

In 2014, Devin and I launched Monday the same way we had launched A Bikini A Day: out of our shared apartment. Our first collection was only ten pieces. We originally promoted it on the A Bikini A Day website and people absolutely loved it, but then, due to the inevitable hiccups that come up when starting any new company (more on that in the next chapter), it took us nearly a year to actually get the brand launched and the products made and into the hands of consumers. I'll never forget those first few days after our original collection of suits arrived. They were shipped to our shared apartment – we didn't pay for any sort of office or storage space, so the living area of our apartment doubled as both – and there was not one square inch of empty space. It was floor-to-ceiling boxes everywhere you looked. Me, Devin, our A Bikini A Day intern and even some of our friends spent days sitting on that floor, sorting through boxes and looking through every piece for quality control. We launched while Devin and I were at Swim Week in Miami, which made sense for the brand, but leaving town meant the intern was left alone at our place to pack and ship orders.

As it turned out, the launch went way better than we'd anticipated, but our intern called us on the day of in a panic: 'There are a hundred orders and I can't do this all by myself,' she said. I remember looking at Devin with fear in my eyes. 'Who can we call to go over there and help out? Do you have any college classmates who would be able to take over?' Devin ended up calling a girl named Ahna, who agreed to go over and help. She walked into our apartment, took charge and seriously saved the day. We didn't know Ahna very well back then, but her generosity with her time and her ability to execute under pressure did not go unnoticed. Today she works as a Monday operations manager, and she's one of Monday's longest-standing employees.

Don't let the hustle porn on social media or TV or movies fool you – there's really nothing sexy about the early days when you're trying to launch your business while keeping costs down. It's scrappy and can involve shipping orders from your living room and packaging products until you have blisters, or responding to customer service complaints from your bed on a Friday night or Sunday morning. So if you're doing this for the city skyline view from your corner office, you might be in for a rude awakening. Our over-packed living room situation stuck around for a while. Eventually we rented the apartment downstairs to double as our office space but not until we had real money coming in. As for hiring help, while you absolutely shouldn't take advantage of anyone, it *is* OK to call in a favour or two. Starting a business is an all-hands-on-deck situation, with the hope and intention that anyone who is willing to help out today will be rewarded for their efforts in the future.

Start small

A lot of young entrepreneurs I talk to tend to 'dream big', and by 'big' I mean bigger than they need to when they're just starting out. They want to skip the 'Steve Jobs in his garage, Tash and Devin on their living room floor' start-up phase and go straight into having an office, or a physical store, multiple employees and custom everything! The smarter way to start a business is to dip your toe in, start small and hustle to grow. How you do that will depend on your business, but here are a few things you can consider to save on costs in the beginning (much of this will be covered in more detail later but is important to keep in mind from the very beginning):

- Work from home if you can, and if your business does require an office, try out a month-to-month shared space.
- Be your own staff. While the stakes are low and your customer base is small you can do more than you might think – don't assume you need to hire someone until you've tried to cover that role yourself.
- Don't invest in unnecessary technology or services. When Jacqui and I started The Pilates Class we launched on a pre-existing video platform that had low fees. Sure, it wasn't as customised as we would have liked but the quality of our content spoke for itself and the platform worked like a charm. Once we had the funds from subscriptions, we built out our own custom app, but that technology can cost hundreds of thousands of dollars. If we had waited to raise that money to start TPC, it may never have got off the ground.
- Forgo customised packaging or other unnecessary branding assets. We all want to present our product in its best light, but – at least in the beginning – go for the classic or cheaper options. There's always a way to present your offering well without spending money unnecessarily. Let your product speak for itself.
- Hire part-time contractors rather than full-time employees on a payroll.
- If your business is product based, purchase only small amounts of inventory.
- Learn to use a camera, and rent equipment to shoot your own content rather than paying a photographer.

The type of business you launch will dictate where you can save and where you want to spend. When Devin and I were building Monday, we spent only on the swimsuits themselves and some small shipping supplies. I invested $30,000 from a personal loan (money I had thanks to my influencer work) into our first collection. Eight years later, when it was time to launch TPC, I once again invested $30,000 from my savings. On that occasion, we didn't even need it all because Jacqui and I did our best to implement all the tips above and keep costs down. We invested mostly in marketing. On the other hand, businesses like A Bikini A Day, and even my production company, I started with little to no financing and built over time.

Quit your day job

There will come a time when it *is* necessary to drop the second job and focus entirely on your own company. But when you're in the heat of launching a business or just trying to keep it afloat – especially if you're juggling that with the second job or whatever work is delivering your actual pay cheque – you may not have a moment to take a step back and think clearly enough to recognise that, as it turns out, that time has come. When it's taking every ounce of your time and attention to maintain the status quo, making big strategic decisions can feel totally overwhelming. But if you set goals ahead of time and determine specific milestones for when it will be time to focus entirely on your business, then you won't have to worry about whether quitting is the responsible and necessary decision or if you're being impulsive or just leaving because you're worn out.

Everyone's individual markers or milestones will be

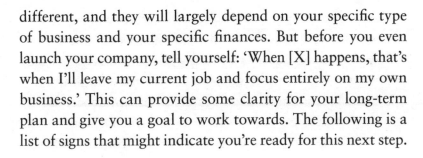

different, and they will largely depend on your specific type of business and your specific finances. But before you even launch your company, tell yourself: 'When [X] happens, that's when I'll leave my current job and focus entirely on my own business.' This can provide some clarity for your long-term plan and give you a goal to work towards. The following is a list of signs that might indicate you're ready for this next step.

1. You can take a liveable wage from the business. As I've said, the longer you can defer taking a salary from your business, the more money you can invest back into the business and the faster you can grow. But there should come a time when you can do both – take a salary and still have plenty to reinvest into growth. You may not want to take as big a salary as you were making at your day job (depending on what your job was and how long you were there), but you need to be sure you can pay yourself enough to cover your living expenses and lifestyle.

2. The business has stable revenue. One or two months of bringing in money isn't enough. Many businesses (like swimsuits!) are seasonal, so it's important to have a fuller picture of the finances than just sales from a single quarter. Set a reasonable time frame for yourself: if you are stable or growing, month over month, for six months or, better yet, a year, then you can feel reasonably safe to leave.

3. You've saved up an emergency fund. Starting a business is risky, and any number of unforeseen things can happen and become a drain on finances, including your business going under. Of course I hope that doesn't happen to you, but it's important to be realistic about your safety net. Before you forgo the outside

pay cheque, you'll want to save up enough to keep you afloat for at least six months, though an even safer bet is to be able to cover your bills for a full year.

4. You have a loyal and engaged customer base. Having a splashy launch and a ton of early orders or subscribers is great, but to really build a business you need to be sure you have repeat customers. That's how companies grow – when consumers keep coming back and tell their friends and share widely. Don't let the early numbers lure you into a false confidence that you're going to be a hit. Instead, wait to ensure that people are returning before you forgo your steady pay cheque.

5. You have a clear plan for growth. Giving up your day job probably means that, for the foreseeable future, you want to dedicate your time to your new business. Hopefully it's a long-term plan, not just a right-now whim. As such, you need to be able to anticipate growth and have an actual long-term business strategy, and not just in your head but in writing. Before you give up the pay cheque, document a one-, three- and five-year plan for how you will scale your business, even if it's just a general outline of where you see the business going, what audiences you want to target, and your ultimate dreams for the business down the line. That way, when you start your new job as a full-time entrepreneur, you know there will be plenty of work to keep you busy and you won't find yourself in a month's time wondering what's next.

3

Believe in yourself, and take risks accordingly

I've been popular and unpopular, successful and unsuccessful, loved and loathed and I know how mean- ingless it all is. Therefore I feel free to take whatever risks I want.

MADONNA

Monday Swimwear, as it exists today, started with me taking the single biggest risk of my career. Devin and I had met with a family-owned swimwear manufacturer who, during Swim Week, approached us about starting our own line of suits. It made sense: at this point we'd worn pretty much every swimwear brand in existence, and we knew what worked and what didn't. But we weren't designers and, quite honestly, we had no idea where to start. The manufacturer, which also operated its own swim retail store, proposed that Devin and I would design the suits; it would produce and sell them.

Devin and I were so excited. We had a clear vision for what

we wanted to create, so we signed a one-year contract and designed an entire collection. There were only about ten pieces in the original line, but still, to go from modelling swimwear on our website to creating our own suits and potentially selling them? It was huge. And we really were excessively obsessed – with our designs but also with the idea of harnessing our passion and turning it into even bigger careers. For our very own swimwear to be sold on a site that already had loyal customers? It was literally a dream come true.

Or so we thought.

In December 2013, once all the pieces in our collection were made, Devin and I went to Australia to shoot the whole line on the beaches of Sydney. It was Christmas Day and there I was in my hometown, with my best friend, taking photographs for my first clothing line (yes, we shot our own campaigns). I could not have asked for a better holiday. But a part of our contract with the manufacturer was that our line would be exclusive to its retail site. It seemed like a fair deal at the time. That is, until the company's buyer, who planned out its inventory and chose what it would buy for its store, decided to buy only certain pieces from our collection. To reiterate: it was a *ten-piece* collection that was exclusive to *one* retailer, but that retailer decided it wanted only some of what we'd made. Which meant we couldn't sell the other pieces anywhere! The retailer bought our cobalt blue bikini top, for example, but then didn't want to buy the matching bottom. What?! It made absolutely no sense. And because it was a big, established swimwear manufacturer and we were just two young women with no design experience, it figured we'd accept the decision, say thank you anyway, and keep our heads down and our mouths shut. Which, quite frankly, is not my style.

Instead, I asked for a meeting with the company, and

we met in a boardroom in its Orange County, California, offices. Something had gone remarkably wrong, we were not OK with it, and we weren't going to pretend otherwise. 'This is not acceptable,' I told them. 'What you've done is counter-intuitive; we didn't work this hard on a collection just to see it pulled apart by your team.'

While I was speaking, the woman with whom I'd originally set up our arrangement started scolding me – 'You don't know what you're talking about; you should feel lucky that we're working with you; this is how these deals work!' – and then stormed out of the boardroom. Honestly, it was strange – but also quite telling. Devin and I were very specific about what we wanted in our line, and this manufacturer was clearly used to pumping out commercial products without the same level of attention to detail. Plus, the way she spoke to us felt like a sign of things to come. How were we going to do business with someone if we couldn't even engage in healthy disagreements? And if she didn't take our expertise seriously? Even then I knew the importance of healthy communication, and so, when she came back into the boardroom, I uttered the four words that even I was surprised to hear coming out of my mouth: 'Maybe this isn't working.' She agreed.

The truth is, we were never a good fit. Devin and I were building Monday as we would if it was entirely our own brand, and this manufacturer was holding us back. But still! At the time, this company held all the cards. It was established in the swim world. It had the means to get a swimsuit produced and sold. We had a bunch of bathing suit designs and a brand that we were excited about – and that we knew our followers were excited about – but no understanding of how to get those designs made or into the hands of consumers.

Despite all these risks, and the vast unknown that lay ahead of us, we walked. Devin and I turned our backs on the biggest deal of our careers and decided to bet on ourselves. The moment we were back in the car, heading home from that fateful meeting, we looked at each other with wide eyes, clearly both wondering the same thing: *What are we going to do now?*

To this day, ending that relationship is the best career decision I've ever made. But we had no backup plan, and now we had a company to run – when we parted ways with the manufacturer we took our designs and the brand with us (which we were lucky to be able to do – any new brand should be aware of these rights) – and we spent the next year figuring it out and learning as we went. We had absolutely no idea what we were doing, but what we lacked in knowledge about the design execution we made up for in our certainty about what we wanted our product to be and how we wanted our company to run. We believed in ourselves and our vision, and so we took a risk rather than play it safe with a manufacturer and retailer that we weren't proud of and didn't have any confidence in.

Starting a business of your own can feel like diving off a cliff again and again and again. The act of launching a company is, in and of itself, a major risk. Research conducted by the global start-up financing network Fundsquire and reported in a January 2019 article in the *Telegraph* found that, in the UK, 20 per cent of small businesses fail within the first year, and 60 per cent fail within the first three years (the global average is pretty much the same). But if you don't believe that the risk is worth it and that your idea will make it, you're already starting from behind.

Let's assume that you *will* be in the group that succeeds – things will still go wrong and hard decisions will still come up as you're building your company, and each time you'll have to listen to your gut and believe in the fact that *you* are the ultimate expert in your brand. Starting a business requires strong confidence and a healthy appetite for risk. Without these, yes, it will be hard to succeed, but it will be even harder to enjoy yourself.

What's wrong with being confident?

I was born with an innate confidence. As a kid, for better or worse, even if I was bad at something, I thought I was great. Today I've honed that a bit. I know what I'm good at, and I'm confident enough in those strengths to recognise where I fall short without questioning myself or falling into a pit of self-doubt. Instead, I hire employees or partner with people who fill in those gaps or act as a complement. My confidence is a quality I value in myself but also in others – my role models have always been defined by their undeniable and unapologetic confidence, and it's what I look for in anyone I surround myself with. In fact, instilling confidence in others is the underlying mission of all my brands. (When you order anything from Monday, it arrives in packaging that literally says, 'Confidence delivered.')

That said, I know it doesn't come easily to everyone, especially women. A 2021 survey of women worldwide, conducted by The Body Shop and reported in its Global Self Love Index, found that one in two women feel more self-doubt than self-love. Other research, conducted by the WealthiHer Network, this time with women in the UK specifically and published in its 2020/21 report *The Changing Faces of Women's Wealth*, found that 79 per cent admitted to struggling with self-esteem. But research also shows that having confidence is critical to entrepreneurial success. Those with higher self-confidence are more likely to be an entrepreneur in the first place, and more likely to be a successful one. It makes sense when you think about it: clients and consumers can sense authenticity. If you don't believe in your company and what it has to offer, why would anybody else? If you don't project an absolute certainty in your ability to lead your brand-new business to a successful outcome, why would any employees want to come on board?

Now, let's be clear. Business confidence doesn't mean that you think you're the very best at everything you do, and I certainly don't want you walking around believing that you're better than other people. That's just called being cocky, which is a very different conversation. But it *does* mean you know your company better than anyone and believe in it whole-heartedly. You need to know your company so well, and believe in its potential so much, that you can speak about it authoritatively at a moment's notice, whether you're at a business meeting or a dinner party or a bridal shower. If you have that level of knowledge and passion, the confidence is a by-product. You aren't stumbling over your words or unsure of your messaging – you're so immersed in the business that you know it by heart. You never know where you're going to meet someone who might be integral to your company's success, so being able to speak passionately and confidently about its potential is key.

Confidence can also be empowering when it comes to taking risks. Many women are scared to take risks because they worry something will go wrong and it will be their fault. Not every risk pays off, or maybe it does in the long run but the immediate outcome is unexpected, and if you lack confidence you might end up blaming yourself. Confidence will help you remember that even if things go wrong, or not the way you planned, it's not personal. If you believe in yourself, you can feel solid in the belief that you made the right decision even if the outcome wasn't what you'd hoped. Not to mention, the fact that admitting that something didn't work takes confidence in itself. There's nothing more impressive than someone who can admit that they tried something, it didn't work out and it's time to move on.

Here's the thing about this kind of confidence: you can't fake it. The minute you start pretending you're something you're not, or pretending you know something you don't, that's when you get nervous. And people can sniff out nerves. They can tell when someone is being phoney. But if you understand a company or an industry inside and out – if you know it better than anyone else – it's easy to talk about it. Devin and I knew swimwear better than anyone when we started Monday. I truly believe that. And today we know every intricacy of the industry and also our company. If one of my employees asked me to jump on a conference call at the last minute, I could go in with no preparation and still have something to contribute once the conversation gets started because it's my brand and I can speak to it with expertise. I may not know the most recent sales data on every suit (though, honestly, I might), but I know where to find it and how to analyse it. I can comment on the numbers historically and their growth over time. I have insight into the competition and how we differentiate ourselves in the market. The point is, I have context and knowledge and I don't doubt myself, because I know that no one knows Monday better than I do.

But just because I don't doubt myself, it doesn't always mean that everyone else is automatically convinced. Yes, your confidence in yourself will inspire others to have confidence in you, and there have been plenty of people who've respected me from the beginning of my career. But I can't deny the fact that I am a business owner with no higher-education degree who also works as an influencer and swimsuit model. To say that I am regularly underestimated would be, well ...

an understatement. We live in a world where there are a lot of stereotypes that might make someone look at a business owner and assume they don't have what it takes – looks, age, even who you know or who your family is. And there is such a stigma around working as an influencer, even if it's a side gig.

Don't be confused, I'm not asking you to feel sorry for me. If anything, I use this to my advantage. If you find that people don't take you seriously, or underestimate your ability, use it to your advantage. Whenever I tell people I own a swimwear company their response is something like, 'Oh, you're cute' – until they hear some of our sales numbers. Fine by me! If someone assumes you won't pose any real competition to their brand, they are much more forthcoming with information and advice.

A final note on confidence: it comes in many forms. For some people, being confident means being the loudest voice in the room, leading discussions and steering decisions. Someone else with similar confidence might prefer to keep quiet and observe, speaking up only when necessary. There is no one way to believe in yourself and your idea, so don't try to contort your personality to fit whatever you think the 'confident business owner' looks like. If your belief in and passion for your idea is genuine, that will come through no matter your personality or communication style.

Seven tips to build your confidence

1. Surround yourself with confident people who build you up and root for your success rather than put you down.
2. Take a public-speaking or acting course. Courses

like this, even if you have no interest in ever being an actor, can help you feel more confident when representing your brand, working with other people and/or speaking in front of them.

3. Check tasks off your to-do list. You can gain a lot of confidence and fulfilment from feeling like you are being productive and getting things done – make a list of even the smallest tasks or duties you need to do and check them off daily.

4. Exercise! Working out to a great playlist and getting your energy up and endorphins going is one of the fastest ways to boost self-confidence.

5. Choose 'your people'. This is a trusted group of individuals whose constructive criticism or feed-back you take seriously. Once you've identified that group, forget about the rest. You can't please everyone and there will always be someone with an opinion, so stop listening so much to what others think and start trusting your own intuition.

6. Go skydiving! OK, maybe not skydiving, but do something that takes you out of your comfort zone and makes you feel alive. It will make the smaller things that scare you feel less significant.

7. Give back. Performing even small gestures of kindness and generosity for others is proven to make you feel more confident and fulfilled within yourself. Try to do one good deed for someone else every day, and give yourself a pat on the back when you do!

Be the owner of your own success

In the earliest stages of starting your business you are going to have some big decisions to make about how much you rely on others and how much you rely on yourself. As with any professional endeavour, you will need help along the way – sometimes that's monetary help, sometimes it's about getting access to someone else's connections or bringing in their skill set. As I've said, understanding where you have gaps and finding the right people to fill them is a necessary part of any entrepreneurial endeavour – no successful venture is built entirely by one person (we'll talk a lot more about building the right team in the next part of this book). But one of the biggest lessons I learned from the blow-up with our original Monday manufacturer is to never put my success in someone else's hands. I signed a deal with that company because it was the first to approach me, and I didn't really know how else to get started. But, by doing so, I handed over a big portion of control – someone else had the power to decide which of my creations to make available to consumers, and that made me so frustrated. There is nothing worse than feeling utterly powerless about something that really should be your call. This was our business and our hands were tied, and I decided then and there that it was the last time I'd let that happen.

Today I rely on my knowledge that I'm the person best suited to seal my own fate and ensure my own success. No one will ever be as invested as you are in the success of your passion project. That's why it's *your* passion. Even if someone else has a monetary stake, if they aren't emotionally invested – meaning they don't feel called to the work, or it's not fulfilling their purpose – they simply won't care as much, because they will always have other projects or backup plans or the next best thing. When you allow someone else to determine your success, you'll often end up disappointed. I fully believe that no one knows what's best for my businesses better than I do. I understand our customers, I believe in my knowledge of what will work, and I'm very confident in my ability to learn what I don't know, or hire the right people or vendors to help in those areas. Remember, I knew nothing about manufacturing a swimsuit when I took the risk of ditching that partnership, and a year later I had a full line of bikinis sitting in my living room. Those suits existed only because Devin and I did the research and asked around and interviewed manufacturers and figured it out.

Once I saw what I could make happen, even without the partnership of some old-guard company that had decades of experience on me, I vowed to always own my own success. It's also why I've never hired an agent to help negotiate my business deals. Frankly, I've never wanted to pay someone 20 per cent of what I earn to answer my emails for me or tell me how much I should be getting paid. I've always known my own worth, and have been willing to put in the work and have the hard conversations necessary to capitalise on my own success. But I'm not going to lie to you: they *are* hard conversations, and I know a lot of people feel uncomfortable advocating and negotiating on their own behalf. I completely understand that, but as a business owner you need to be able to represent yourself every day, so get the practice where you can.

Maintaining control doesn't mean you should microman-age every little decision or day-to-day task, but the buck should stop with you. If you don't like the way something is being done, you should have the power to change it. Today, Monday is a direct-to-consumer website, which means we don't have to rely on a buyer to choose which of our products are sold or featured on its retail site. Devin and I make that call. Since walking out on that company, I have always been responsible for my success, and the success of my companies. That doesn't mean everything always goes perfectly, but when things go wrong I don't have regrets. I don't wonder if I could have handled it better. If you're obsessed enough with an idea that you are willing to leave a steady job or take on a second one just to get that idea up and running, then you better believe that you are the best person to make the final calls about the major decisions. If you have the idea but don't trust yourself to execute, then you're only halfway to the finish line.

Risky business

As I said earlier, entrepreneurism is inherently risky. Most start-up companies don't make it through the first three years, and nine out of ten fail within a decade. According to market intelligence firm CB Insights' 2021 report *The Top 12 Reasons Startups Fail*, an analysis of 111 start-up post-mortems between 2018 and 2021, some of the most common reasons that businesses fail include lack of financing or cash running out, disharmony among team members and burnout. I don't share these statistics to scare you but because I want you to go into this adventure with a solid sense of what's to come. I want you to believe in your idea but also have a full understanding of the challenges ahead. Chances are, if you're seriously considering pursuing your own business, you already consider yourself a risk-taker. A 2018 poll conducted by the small-business insurance firm Insureon found that around 75 per cent of entrepreneurs identify as risk-takers, while research from Louisiana State University has found that those who are more willing to take risks are nearly 20 per cent more likely to be entrepreneurs.

What if you have an idea you really believe in, but your risk tolerance isn't quite there yet? First, let's take a minute to define what we mean by risk. People often hear that word and picture someone walking up to a roulette wheel, putting all their money on the line, crossing their fingers and hoping it lands on black. But when I say you have to be OK with risk to be a business owner, I mean that you have to be comfortable with some level of uncertainty. If you take a job as an employee at an established company, you can pretty much rely on the fact that you will get a pay cheque every month (or whatever your company's pay schedule is). Of course, nothing is guaranteed in life – even long-standing companies go under and lay-offs happen, and 100 per cent job security is just not a thing these days – but taking on a paid role in someone else's organisation allows a good level of certainty that you will have a steady income. When you start a new business, however, so much is uncertain: how long the business will survive, whether you will bring in revenue, when you will be able to take a salary, if your idea will resonate with consumers . . . the list goes on. But again, you're not just hoping for the best, you are betting on yourself. The risk is *calculated*, meaning you've considered the various uncertainties and the factors involved, and while you can't guarantee an outcome, you know what you are getting into and you believe in your ability to move the outcome in your desired direction. There is likely to be some luck involved along the way, but it's not so much a leap of faith as it is a vote of confidence in yourself. As Oprah once said, 'I believe luck is preparation meeting opportunity. If you hadn't been prepared when the opportunity came along, you wouldn't have been lucky.'

This is important, because I don't want anyone reading this to make a crazy, thoughtless decision and chalk it up to 'I'm a risk-taker!' Don't go jumping out of a plane without a parachute and say that I sent you. In fact, as much as you can mitigate risk in business – like keeping that second job for as long as you can – I'm all for it. But there's a difference between the abject fear that comes along with taking a truly scary risk, one where you have absolutely no control or input and have to cross your fingers and hope for the best, and the kind of excited nerves that come with taking a risk you believe in, and one that can pay off in the end. If I don't have those excited nerves for a while, that's how I know I'm not doing anything that interests or challenges me and I need to find my next pursuit. You'll be able to feel the difference in your gut, and also in your heart, I promise.

At the end of the day, if you simply can't stomach the fact that it's possible you could do everything right and your big idea still might not take off, then maybe starting a business isn't your calling. But if you're reading this and thinking, *I really, truly want to take this chance, I'm just scared of the uncertainty*, the answer might be as simple as revisiting your self-confidence and some of the tips in Chapter 2 (keeping your day job, building your emergency fund). Because if everything else about starting a business sounds great – the long hours, the hard work, the all-eyes-on-you – then you may regret never even giving it a shot. Remember, there should be no better bet than a bet on yourself, and no better feeling than when *your* intuition and hard work pay off.

It's OK to ask

We've already talked about the importance of bartering – asking for one thing in exchange for another – but sometimes when you're in business you simply have to ask for help, or a favour. You may have nothing to offer in return, at least not at the moment, and have to rely on someone's goodwill. Other times you might ask for something because you think you deserve it or because you simply think it's a good idea for everyone involved. But, for some people, directly asking for something is scary. As far as I'm concerned, asking for what you need is not a risk, it's a requirement. Especially in business. The worst-case scenario is that you get a no. And sure, making a request – be it for a loan or a partnership or even an upgrade at a hotel – does involve some level of uncertainty, because you can't be sure what the answer will be. But, of course, if you *don't* ask, you don't get … that is entirely certain.

Before you even launch your business, you will (and should) have a lot of asks of other people. *Can I use our living room as an office space? Would you mind following or commenting on my new social feeds? Will you help me shoot a marketing campaign? Will you be in a focus group for my new app? Can I have a discount on your service until my business is up and running?* As I've said, no business is built alone, but there are so many scenarios in life – especially business scenarios – where we think we're supposed to manage it all on our own and that it's not appropriate to ask for any help. Women, especially, worry about seeming needy or demanding. We worry that asking for things is inappropriate, but let me be clear: asking for something politely and clearly is not entitled, it's called communication! It's how businesses are built. I don't think there is a single successful business in the world that could honestly claim it got to where it is today without ever asking anything of anyone. You have to talk to other business owners and put yourself out on a limb in order to make connections and build partnerships and learn the ropes of your field. It may feel risky – especially if the person you're asking is more experienced or established in your industry – but I bet you will be surprised the number of times people say yes.

From the very beginning of my business career I was willing to ask anyone for anything. I didn't make demands or act like I deserved special treatment, but if I needed a hand from a friend, I asked for it. If I had an idea for a partnership, even if it seemed far-fetched, I made the pitch. Some of our biggest brand partnerships came from moments where we thought, *It's hard to imagine this giant company would want to work with us, but why not ask?* That was certainly the case in 2017 when we partnered with Guess for a campaign and capsule collection. I think it was the biggest partnership Guess did that year, other than a collab with rapper A$AP Rocky, and it was all because I wrote to them and put the question out there: 'Would you be interested in collaborating? I think Guess and A Bikini A Day would be a natural fit, and here's why ...' I didn't even let myself *think* something like *A big company like Guess wouldn't want us.* Instead, I asked myself, *What if there's someone at Guess who believes in us and vibes with us? Might as well find out!* Next thing we knew we were on a world tour promoting the range of swimwear in the storefronts of Guess locations across the globe.

Behind every great brand or business are actual people – human beings that have the power to make things happen, and have likes and dislikes and opinions on what and who they believe in. You never know when someone behind the scenes at a brand will personally believe in you and even advocate for you. Shoot your shot! At the end of the day, business is all about creating relationships, and asking for something is a great conversation starter. This is where you start building the connections that will pay off throughout the lifespan of your business and career.

The willingness to ask for things is another place where confidence and risk intersect. Because before you put yourself out there and request whatever it is you want or need, you have to believe you *deserve* that thing. Let's say you show up at a hotel, and the room you are assigned looks nothing like the room you thought you'd booked. What do you do? Accept the lesser room because you're scared to ask for better? No, you go and ask directly but politely, 'Is there a different room available? The one I'm in looks very different from what I booked online and I'm paying a lot and am on holiday, so I would love a room with a view.' One commonality between all successful people, I've found, is that they set a certain standard for themselves and then they ask for what they want because they truly believe they are up to that standard. They expect the best for themselves and work for it. And that's as true for a business partnership as it is a hotel room. Devin and I believed our company could be on the level of a global empire like Guess, so we weren't nervous and apologetic when we made the ask. We didn't say, 'We know we're just a little company but ...' We came in and communicated as if we were equals, and that confidence made a big difference to both parties.

Never is the 'asking' phase more important than in the earliest days of your business, when you have no revenue, few (if any) employees and nothing to show for yourself yet in terms of a loyal consumer following. But every time you think of making an ask as a risk, I want you to replace the word 'risk' with 'responsibility'. Because that's the truth. If you really want to be a leader and a business owner, it's your responsibility to go after what you want and what your company needs. And the earlier you conquer your nerves and start enquiring as necessary, the sooner your business will be the success you know it can be.

PART 2

How to execute

4

Finding a partner, building a team

Great things in business are never done by one person, they are done by a team of people.

STEVE JOBS

Entrepreneurial success can't be tied to any one thing – it's a combination of hard work, timing, luck and a huge number of other factors – but if I had to pick one variable that is critical no matter what type of business you're trying to build, I would point, every time, to relationships. Ultimately, every business is just a group of people, working together in the hope of creating something that matters. And what most people want, when it comes right down to it, is to be respected, inspired and treated well. If you can get this part right – and the earlier the better – you're already a step ahead.

Of course, before a business is a *group* of people, it starts off as one or two people. Maybe you came up with the idea together, like Devin and I did that night in our tiny apartment, when A Bikini A Day was born. Maybe you're the one who came up with the idea, but it relies on someone else's particular skills, as happened with The Pilates Class, when I saw the potential in Jacqui's style of teaching Pilates online. Or maybe the idea is all yours, and now you need to decide if you want to pursue it independently or take on a business partner. Figuring out if you want to work with someone else, and how you will approach the partnership, is step number one when it comes to executing your idea.

In general, I prefer to work with a business partner when I launch a new venture. Ideally, we have different but complementary strengths, which means we can divide and conquer when it comes to work responsibilities and assignments. Since I prefer not to take on external investors when I start a company, having someone I can bounce ideas off and get input from is invaluable.

Business partnerships can be tricky. Sometimes you get incredibly lucky and stumble into a relationship that becomes a best friendship and a business partnership and it feels like it was meant to be all along. That's what happened with Devin and me – a decade after meeting and launching a business together she was my maid of honour, and the swimsuit company we co-founded is doing multimillions in revenue. But our story is the exception rather than the rule – finding the right partner can be incredibly complicated – and even in our case there have been some rare moments of conflict or tension and even tears. Which is why today I am incredibly selective regarding who I go into business with, because when the partnership works out it can be a huge benefit to your business, but when it goes wrong, your business can go very south, very quickly.

Finding your other half

Let's say you decide you want to go into business with someone else. Choosing your business partner might be a no-brainer, for all the reasons I've already stated – it was their idea, or you need their talent. But let's say you have a great idea and you want to launch a company around it, but you consider yourself a creative. You don't know much about crunching numbers and creating budgets, and you don't particularly want to learn, either. Or you *do* want to learn (every entrepreneur needs to know this stuff, I promise), but you don't feel comfortable taking charge of the financials just yet. After all, you want this company to succeed, and you know your own weaknesses. How do you go about finding the right partner? What should you look for? Here are some dos and don'ts:

- **You don't want another you.** It's tempting to want to work with someone who seems similar and familiar to you, I get that. But your business already has you! You will better serve the company, the customers and eventually your employees by choosing someone with a different set of skills, whether that refers to tactical skills (you're good at marketing, they're great at business strategy; you are the ideas person while they are the number cruncher) or soft skills (you are a great communicator and inspiring leader; they are decisive and can keep calm in moments of chaos). You might also want someone with a different work or educational background. If you've spent your career thus far working in a creative field, someone with a corporate background will complement your experience. Maybe you bring in someone with a business degree who can handle the day-to-day logistics of running a company so that you free yourself up to work on the marketing or design side of things.

- **You do need the same business values and vision.** If you want to create a true business partnership, then you and your co-founder will need to make big decisions together. Aligning your values and vision should be top of your priority list, as it can really make or break your partnership. If one of you wants to run at a loss in favour of fast growth while the other would prefer a slow, steady build in order to preserve funds, that's a conflict in vision, and it will make running a company and making strategic decisions together very difficult. Talk openly about how you envision running a company, and your goals for the next one, three and five years, *before* you sign on any dotted lines.
- **You don't need to be best friends.** Yes, Devin, Jacqui and I are, but like I said, we're an exception. You are going to work closely with this person and go through crazy stressful moments and late nights in the office and painful rejections together, so you need to respect them and enjoy their company because otherwise the hard times will seem downright impossible. But you don't need to be best friends outside of the office, and more often than not, you probably shouldn't be. If the partnership doesn't work out, the friendship can be really hard to save.
- **You do need to believe in and admire their skill set.** If your partnership relies on the understanding that you each handle different 'departments' of the business, then there will be times when you need to defer to the

other person. You might have an opinion on something they are doing, but ultimately if there are areas that your partner 'owns' then they make the final call on relevant decisions, which is why it's critically important that you genuinely respect and admire whatever it is that your business partner is good at (and they feel the same about you). If you're constantly second-guessing them, or thinking *I would have done it differently/ wouldn't have made that mistake/could do their job better*, your resentment is going to build a lot faster than your company will. A big reason why many partnerships fail is due to bruised egos and power plays, so avoid them at all costs.

- **You do need to have honest, open communication.** If you and your business partner can't be candid with each other and speak truthfully, then it's really not a partnership at all. There are going to be hard conversations – about equity, about the future of the business, about partnerships or hiring, about budget – and if you're worried that you can't talk openly to this person, or if you get the sense that they aren't being transparent with you, it will feel impossible to move forwards. My business partners and I can switch back and forth between serious negotiations and light-hearted discussions in the blink of an eye. We always know we want what's best for each other and best for the company. I'm someone who generally says what's on my mind, and I have been since I was a kid, which definitely helps me in my role as an entrepreneur. If you have trouble asserting yourself or saying what's on your mind, then I encourage you to work on that *before* you decide to launch a business. It will make any business partnership hard, but the truth is even starting a company on your own will be hard. Eventually you'll need employees, and no one wants a leader who is too timid to lead.

So where do you find this person? Don't limit yourself to friends or people you know well. Someone you've worked with in the past can be a great option. Maybe there is someone you went to college with who has a complementary skill set. Maybe a neighbour. If you put it out into the universe that you are looking for a partner, and you keep your eyes and ears open, you'll be surprised how many potential business partners cross your path.

Figuring out your piece of the pie

One of the earliest conversations you and your would-be business partner need to have is about equity. How much of the business will each of you own? Before you immediately say, 'We'll split it 50/50', take a moment to consider what each person is contributing, and how much of their time they are dedicating to the business. I recently spoke to a woman hoping to launch a venture with two other partners. When I asked her the plan for equity she said, 'We're just going to split it three ways.' Well, OK, except one person is a freelance designer who can continue to do their independent work on the side, while another – the woman I was talking to – is the head of a department at a giant company, who will be giving up a high six-figure pay cheque to start the company, not to mention the fact that she'll bring a Rolodex of major companies she already has relationships with. I'm sure they will both work hard to create a successful venture, but the value of what each person is bringing to the company is different, and they should be compensated accordingly. All too often the go-to plan is to just slice the pie evenly, and that's usually because it feels too awkward to negotiate what you might really be worth.

What is equity and how does it work?

Equity, at its most basic level, is how much of the business a person owns, usually expressed as a percentage. If you launch a business with a partner, and you split the company evenly and don't take on any investors, then you would each own 50 per cent of the business – you each have 50 per cent of the equity. But you may decide that your contributions aren't equal and that you will split the equity 60/40 or 70/30. This is perfectly common. If you take on investors, they will get equity in exchange for their funding. Basically, by bank-rolling your business, investors are buying a percentage of ownership (how much that percentage is worth in actual cash depends on what you determine the value of your company to be). In a start-up company, equity is critically important. You may not have any profit yet, but once you do, your equity in the company will determine how much of that profit you are entitled to. If you have a business idea and want to bring on employees but don't yet have the funds to offer a competitive salary, you can offer a small piece of the company – equity – to make your offer more attractive. If a business doesn't take off, the equity may not amount to much, but if it *does*, it can translate to a big payday.

These conversations can get tricky, there's no doubt about that. Talking about money is complicated, especially explaining to someone why you think you deserve more than they do. My ownership in my companies has changed over time because circumstances change, and I'm lucky to have teamed up with partners who are open to difficult conversations and getting real about who is pulling more or less weight.

When I talked to my friend, the one who is starting her new company, my message was clear: know your worth, don't undersell yourself, and ask for what you deserve. And also, leave your ownership open to negotiation. There's so much you can't anticipate when you first jump in, so after six months or so, you may have a better sense of who is doing what and also who deserves what. There's nothing wrong with re-evaluating once you have more information.

Figuring out the breakdown of who deserves what gets harder and harder as you bring more people into your business, but sometimes that trade-off is worth it. Sure, you get a smaller piece of the pie, but in exchange you bring in people who are adding real value to your company. And, remember, getting 50 per cent of a company that's worth $100,000 is a lot less than getting 25 per cent of a company that's worth $1 million, so if bringing in additional partners will significantly increase your company's value, it's worth it. Still, it's important to understand the implications of growing your ownership team.

Maybe you want to start a tech company, and you have a friend that does coding, an acquaintance who does finance and another friend who does graphic design. You can save a lot of money in the beginning if you bring those people on board and split their equity according to how valuable their skill sets are to the company. This may help get the company off the ground faster and for less money, which means you'll make more, as a business, sooner. However, by bringing all these people on board, you've diluted your equity and will own a smaller chunk of the business. This might be necessary for you – maybe you're up against a deadline or other competition that means your time to market is pivotal – but if you're in a position to go slow, build organically and bring in fewer partners, you may be better off. After all, as I've mentioned, everyone with ownership in a company has the right to an opinion about how you do things. And that's great if you're all in agreement, or if you've clearly laid out the terms of your partnership with a lawyer to start. But if you don't all have the same ideas about how to build your company, or you haven't clearly communicated your visions from the outset, these bigger ownership teams can lead to conflict, and lots of it.

Moral of the story: yes, conversations about money and ownership are tricky, but you need to have them quickly and clearly – and potentially repeatedly – if you are going to own a business with someone. If you've divvied up the company fairly, you will all be working towards the same goals and have a fair stake in the company's achievements. At that point, you will genuinely want success, happiness and fulfilment for your business partners as much as you want those things for yourself, and eventually that will extend to everyone who is a part of your business and your network.

Of course, not every partnership will work out. Just like any relationship, even one that is great for a while can run its course. You may find that a business partner has lost interest in the company or isn't pulling their weight. You may disagree on your goals for the business or the ways in which you want to move forwards once you find a bit of success. You may take different approaches to hiring employees or have different views on work culture. And sometimes a relationship you think is going to work out isn't what you expect. You may both sign on the dotted line full of energy and enthusiasm, but it turns out your communication styles don't match up or that you second-guess each other's handling of finances. I have absolutely entered into partnerships that haven't been the right fit – sometimes your excitement about a product can get the better of you and suddenly you realise you're in business with someone you shouldn't be, for whatever reason. In this scenario, it's better to cut your losses sooner rather than later. Hopefully you'll have learned or gained something from the partnership regardless (even if it's just understanding the types of partnerships that don't work for you – very important info to know!), but when I'm in doubt, I like to set myself a six-month window to consider whether I want to be in or out. If things don't improve in that time frame, I make a change. I know some people that stay in partnerships they shouldn't be in for *years* just because they feel like they have to. You don't! Yes, you have to give it your best shot, but don't let guilt or shame hold you back from letting something go that's not serving you. Particularly if the relationship is all give and no take. That's just bad business. And the sooner you cut ties, the better shot you have at preserving the relationship or ending on good terms if that is important to you. The longer bad feelings fester, the more you will suffer resentment. Your time is your biggest asset, so be sure to protect it and use it wisely.

The one-woman show

When your company first launches, it's likely to be just you and your business partner(s), doing it all. Need to fulfil an order? You're there with the packing tape. Need to post on social? You're the brand ambassador. Need to update your website? You'll log into Squarespace. It can be exhausting to spend so much time on parts of the business that have nothing to do with your passion, and I know that because I did it. In the early days of Monday, I shipped the box, I did customer service, I handled the quality control. Many entrepreneurs will say the same. You can't be too good for any task when you're trying to build a brand and keep costs down. And as frustrating as it was to be the IT and HR person when all I wanted to be doing was designing swimsuits and making big, important business decisions, it turned out to be a real blessing. All these years later, I make it a point to have a thorough understanding of nearly every job required in any company I start, and would suggest any entrepreneur – *especially* any first-time entrepreneur – do the same. As the company grows and you hire people with more expertise, it may not be realistic for you to be hands-on with every role, but it's important to have a firm grasp of what the experts you bring on are doing.

First of all, having first-hand experience or a general understanding of every role in your company will better equip you to hire the right people when the time comes to build a team. It's hard to choose the right person for a position if you have no idea what the job actually requires. Sure, you can look at a CV and previous experience and make your best guess, but every company is so different that until you've taken a turn as, say, social media manager, you won't know what the role demands at your specific business. Is the most important thing posting creative content at a specific time? Or knowing how to deal with a disgruntled customer commenting on your post?

And when the time comes that you don't have to do everything, and you've hired the right people for each role, your experience with each position will inform how you approach your role as a leader. You'll have a strong sense of which areas of the business you need to stay involved in, and where you can delegate and step back. You'll also understand what to expect of each employee – which will come in very handy when it's time to evaluate their performance.

Above all, your experience working in every department of your company will make you a better leader. Once you've built a team, you'll have a keen understanding of how every employee contributes to the whole, which will make you a more appreciative and compassionate boss. How often do you hear a friend complain about their boss or manager, and they say something like, 'They give me a hard time for not doing this or that, but they could never do my job?' or 'They don't even understand what I do!' Your employees will respect you more if they know you've stood in their shoes. Plus, you'll have an even more complete understanding of how your company works.

Knowing how each job is done really will give you credibility with your employees – advice on how to execute a position is far better received when it comes from a place of experience and knowledge than a place of 'If I were to do your job, here is how I would do it better'. But that doesn't mean you should constantly remind someone that you once did what they do now. Once you hire the people that you believe fit the job requirements in each department, it's time to delegate and trust that they will do the job you hired them for. Just because you have experience, doesn't mean you should micromanage. At least not if you want to keep those good employees you worked so hard to find.

Hire power

There are many different approaches to hiring employees, and plenty of opinions on best practices when it comes to building your company, but what I know for certain is that in both of my businesses, one of my greatest successes has been my ability to attract and hire a dream team. When the time comes that you are ready to start bringing on employees, it's important to have a sense of what you're looking for before you even conduct your interviews. Sure, someone who is the exact opposite of what you thought you wanted might blow you away – and if that happens, trust your gut! – but, in general, understanding your priorities when it comes to hiring will help you make hard decisions when you've met a number of great candidates.

When I'm hiring employees for a new company, I'm less interested in previous experience and more interested in a person's attitude, willingness to learn and potential to be a team player. Our current head of marketing for The Pilates Class, Casey, is a great example. Her background isn't in marketing at all. In fact, she started her career as a special effects make-up artist for movies, but there just wasn't enough work in that industry in Sydney, where she lives, so many years ago she volunteered at our A Bikini A Day pop-up shop. Six months later, I was looking for a part-time assistant in Sydney, so I asked my friend Whitney, who'd run the pop-up, if she had anyone to recommend. Whitney didn't know Casey personally, but she remembered her work ethic. 'There was this one girl who stood out,' she said. 'Anything I asked her to do she just got down to business and got it done, no questions asked.' I ended up calling Casey and hiring her on the spot, and she pretty quickly went from part-time assistant to full-time, then she became an intern for The Pilates Class, then head of social media, and now she is the global head of marketing and she's killing it – travelling the world, creating incredible partnerships and helping to build a global fitness brand. I think she'd be the first to tell you she never expected to do this kind of work, but her attitude on that day she worked at the pop-up stood out. Tactical skills can be taught, but being a hard worker and great collaborator and a get-shit-done type of person ... that's more innate, and if you find it in someone, you want that person on your team. (It's a good reminder, too, that you never know who's watching, so no matter where you are working, do what you can to stand out! It could lead to some incredible things you didn't even know you wanted.)

As much as I can, I try to hire employees who double as our customers. You want your team to understand the consumers they're speaking to, so it helps a lot when they *are* those people. This is especially true when you're hiring for marketing or social media roles, but I would argue it's the case across the board. People who understand your brand and purchase your product or subscribe to your service can also serve as an early focus group as you grow and expand your offerings. This is why diversity in hiring is critically important. If you have a diverse team, you have people on board who can speak to and represent your different audiences – regarding race and ethnicity and sexual orientation and gender but also fashion sense or body type or whatever other diversity exists in your customer base. In the early-ish days of Monday, when we wanted to do market research, we always started with our employees, so having our audience represented in our office was invaluable. Given that the target market of my brands is so wide, almost any woman could be a loyal customer, which was incredibly beneficial when it came to hiring. If your brand is targeted to a very niche or specific audience, for example Gen Z only, you will need to ensure that you have at least one or two people representing that demographic in your team that you listen to closely.

Above all else, the number one thing I want in an employee

is loyalty and dedication to the company. Of course, that's something that has to be earned by the organisation. No employee will be blindly dedicated to an employer without getting some dedication in return. But when I say loyalty, I don't mean that the employee never leaves or gets another job. People move around and take other positions – that's how careers are built and it's totally fair. Losing employees is a natural part of running a business, and it never worries me, because if you're a good leader and have a good brand, the next person you attract might be even better. When I talk about company loyalty, I'm talking about the person who will never respond to a request by saying, 'That's not my job.' They're willing to jump in and help wherever they are needed. *Your* responsibility, as a business owner and leader, is to create a culture that inspires this loyalty. That starts by ensuring that everyone you add to the team brings something positive to the work culture. The hope is that your employees have many differences, and yet they share and connect over one common goal: the success of your vision.

Leadership principles

One thing most people don't think about when they decide to start a company is the fact that, if the company succeeds, they are going to need to manage a team. But, if you're lucky, your business will grow and leadership will become a critical aspect of your role as business owner. You may start out with two employees and one day have a hundred people who all funnel up to you, so understanding what it takes to inspire people to do their best work, believe in the company's mission and feel loyal to your brand is non-negotiable. It's easy to think, *Oh, I'm great in relationships, I'll be a great leader*, but managing people well in a professional setting is a specific skill set. It's very different from being a good friend or colleague. You have to educate yourself in advance, whether that happens through training and courses, reading books and listening to podcasts, or asking other business leaders for tips and advice. I like to surround myself with business owners in all different categories – even if you work in completely separate industries, most business owners deal with similar issues and you'll be surprised how much you can learn from someone even if you are in fashion and they are in tech, or you're building a service and they run a product-based business. Bloomberg has become my favourite TV channel; business podcasts are my favourite workout soundtrack. There is something to be learned – about leadership *and* about business – from every interview or conversation with a business owner that you can find. Don't underestimate how important this type of education is, because it really can be the difference between a successful company and a failed one. You don't need to go to college to know how to run a successful business, but you do have to stay curious and be eager to keep learning. And that kind of attitude can be contagious. After all, the culture of a company trickles down from the top, and I always say you have to be whatever it is you want to attract. If you are a leader known for your passion for your brand, your willingness to listen to ideas and your desire to create good work experiences for your employees, you will get that in return. If, on the other hand, you are a poor leader, you will attract poor employees and create a bad culture, and in the end you probably won't have a great brand either. It really is that simple.

Research shows that bad leadership reduces employee productivity and increases turnover. According to a survey from Harvard Business School published in 2015 in the *Harvard Business Review*, some of the most common complaints when it comes to bad leadership are not recognising or giving credit for hard work, giving unclear direction, having no time for employees and not offering constructive criticism. As you can see from that list, employees aren't focused on their bosses being super nice or fun (though there's nothing wrong with those things if you can keep it professional), they want someone who can lead, teach and inspire them.

In my experience there are six important aspects to being a good leader, so I've come up with some rules that help guide me and also make the expectations clear for my team:

1. **I'll teach you anything once.** People in a job want to learn. In fact, it's usually when the learning stops that they get bored and look to move on to a new job and new challenge. I always want to foster an environment of curiosity and growth, so I'm very clear with my team that if there's something you want to learn how to do, I am happy to teach you. But I'll only show you once, so take notes.

2. **There will be mistakes.** Employees are human beings. They aren't going to get everything right all the time. When I say I'll only teach you something once, I mean it – but I don't mean I'm going to get furious or fire you if you get something wrong. Not even close. Laid-back reactions make people feel good, and there's got to be room for human error. But when mistakes happen, I simply challenge my employees to learn from them and then find a way to course-correct. It's in those moments of problem-solving that the most valuable learning happens. If the same mistake happens over and over and over? Well, that's a different story and might be an indication of a larger problem. But as long as it's not intentional and people are doing their best

for themselves and by the company ... what else can you really ask for?

3. **I will always be straight with you.** Nobody in the workplace benefits by avoiding hard conversations, and your responsibility as a leader is to provide honest feedback to your employees. That can feel especially tricky at a small company where you might have close or personal relationships with the people on your team. But if someone isn't doing good work, or is doing something wrong, you owe it to them to be honest, and then give them a chance to improve. Employees need to be open to constructive criticism, but you have to be open to giving it.

4. **I will acknowledge my weaknesses and solve for them.** Just because you're the founder or leader of the business doesn't mean you do everything perfectly. Every single one of us has strengths and weaknesses, and if you're reading this thinking, *Sorry, not me ...* well, I can pretty much guarantee your employees have a different opinion about that! As a leader, it's on you to recognise what aspects of leadership are hardest for you, and rather than think, *Well, they'll just have to deal with it, I'm the boss!*, you need to figure out how *you* can improve or delegate. I, for example, have learned that I'm very good at managing a team of about ten people. I have the bandwidth to get to know that many people so that they understand how I communicate – which is usually efficient and to the point – and won't misconstrue my matter-of-fact delivery as anything negative or personal. When the team at Monday had grown to twenty people, it became clear to me that I wasn't able to lead in the way I wanted because I couldn't cultivate a relationship

with each employee. I'm not great at remembering to say 'How was your weekend?', for example, because I'm always focused on the work at hand and have so much on my plate. If you know me and have worked closely with me, you'll know that's just how I operate and it's nothing personal. If you haven't worked closely with me, however, you might take it the wrong way – as a sign that I don't like you or that you're doing something wrong. This is common with many business owners and managers. I realised when our team grew that I was no longer able to inspire the employees the way I wanted to and give individualised attention, so I hired a general manager who could do what I couldn't because I want to ensure my team always feels valued, no matter how big our company gets.

5. **I will give credit where it's due.** Giving praise is so important. Offering recognition, ideally in some public way, has so much value. If we are in a meeting for The Pilates Class, for example, and I'm presenting a new trainer to the team, I will always point out that, say, Casey found this person, if that's the case. It's a small thing, but it makes an employee feel seen and valued. And because it's a relatively small thing, it's an easy one. Being a good leader doesn't have to mean making grand gestures or giving your employees new cars.
It will cost you nothing to give public credit to good work and make your employee feel appreciated. And it will pay back tenfold if it engenders a dedication to the company, which it often does.

6. **The team will come first.** If you want to earn the respect of your employees, make it crystal clear that their wellbeing is a top priority. I want everyone who works for me to see their job as a career, because I

want them to be invested in the company long term,
so I treat them like career professionals. That starts
with making sure everyone is paid fairly and has good
benefits. It also entails working with employees directly
to give feedback and help them move forwards, and
also to discuss what their future at the company could
look like as they grow. What do you expect from them
in the first year, and what do you envision for them
down the line? This plants the idea of progress in the
employee's mind.

Parenting experts will say that kids actually *want* discipline
and boundaries, they just don't know it, and employees are
similar. They find it inspiring when a boss is paying attention
and providing guidance and support. Although as important
as it is to provide input on your employees' performance, it's
equally important to listen to them and be receptive to *their*
feedback. I truly believe the number one way we've earned
the respect of our Monday and TPC employees is by always
listening to them, whether they are giving input on products
or services, or expressing that they want more flexibility to
work from home.

People management 101 and the six-lane highway worker

I never truly understood the complexity of human beings
until I started managing a team. Everyone has a different
personality, a different working style and a different way of
communicating. One way is not *better* than another, and
many different working styles can add value to your team.
But one of the biggest mistakes you can make as a business

leader is to expect everyone on your team to conform to blanket expectations and fit neatly inside a box. As the leader and manager, it's up to you to recognise who is what type of worker and tailor your expectations accordingly. You could lose a lot of sleep obsessing over what certain employees *could* or *should* be doing, but if your expectations aren't in line with who that person is and what type of worker they are, and you're expecting everyone to bend to what you want, you will be continually disappointed. Successful leadership requires flexibility. If you shift your mindset towards celebrating what each person is good at and moulding expectations around their strengths, more will get done and it will feel easier and more natural for everyone.

As I see it, employees usually fit into one of three buckets: the one-lane highway worker, the three-lane highway worker or the six-lane highway worker. These buckets ultimately correlate with someone's ability to shift focus and handle tasks in different areas of the business, as well as their willingness or desire to take risks and be a leader. Understanding where someone falls, and working with them with that context in mind, has become one of my best team-management tools.

If you've ever driven a car in Los Angeles, you'll know that there are different types of drivers on the busiest expressways. Some people drive on a six-lane highway in LA and they are so on edge and rattled by the experience that you can feel their stress and hesitance even if you are driving behind them or next to them. Then there are the drivers who know what they're doing, and drive responsibly and competently. And then there are the ones who are bobbing and weaving, switching lanes and exuding confidence. Understanding my employees in the context of these categories has been a game changer for my businesses – it allows me to meet my employees where they are and set them up for whatever success looks like to them. Problems only arise when you expect six-lane highway performance from a one-lane highway worker or try to force them to be a six-lane thinker when it's never going to happen. Let me explain . . .

The one-laner

The one-laner is just that – they have one lane, and they like to stay in it. This person has a defined role, they understand their duties in that role, and they rarely veer outside those clear expectations. They may be able to collaborate with another team member, but they generally work better on their own tasks. A one-laner is systematic and lives by their to-do list – they like to have a task at hand and then tick things off. As a result, if you ask them to do something extra and outside their usual job description, they might struggle, because they aren't used to thinking or problem-solving outside their lane. One-lane workers are often really great at what they do. They don't spread themselves too thin and they know what they're capable of, but what they do they do very well.

The one-lane worker is not someone who is keen to take a risk, and if they do they are usually pretty nervous about it. A lot of business thinkers tend to look down on the idea of the one-lane worker because they like using words like *agile* or *nimble* to describe the ideal employee. But there's absolutely nothing wrong with having a worker who stays in their lane, and usually it's the *leader* who needs to adjust their expectation, not the employee. As long as I am clear that someone really thrives in their one lane, I can help them be successful in that space.

There's a lot to be said for an employee who is happy in their lane. They might not climb the ranks of the company, but that may not even be something they aspire to. That said, if they have expressed a desire to progress and grow, don't be afraid to gently push them in that direction. With good guidance and support, a one-laner can become a three-laner, but you need to be clear with them, and that might mean saying, 'I know this is uncomfortable but I also know it's what you want and will eventually make you feel fulfilled, so let's work on it together.'

The three-laner

In my experience, most workers fall into the three-lane bucket. They can think a bit more broadly and outside the box than a one-lane worker, they can pivot more easily and they're better at collaborating with other departments. These employees are learning to think strategically outside their role and are passionate about the bigger picture, so you can throw a couple of random tasks at them and feel confident they'll get them done, but they may not take a ton of initiative when it comes to trying new things. They wait to be instructed or will ask for an assignment. They might have new ideas, but they don't quite see the bird's-eye view of the business just yet.

The three-lane worker needs strong leadership – they want to grow, and usually do so with the support of a manager who can help them flourish. They want the reassurance of someone saying 'Good job!' because when they take a risk – which they will from time to time – they aren't completely confident about it. They want to be told that what they've done was right before they will do it again. Just as a one-lane worker can become a three-laner, a three-laner can grow to a six-laner ... but they won't get there without close mentorship.

The six-laner

If you are going to be a business owner, it's ideal if you are a six-lane highway person, because it encompasses seeing the big picture, thinking strategically and moving seamlessly between departments with an ability to speak to anyone and understand their goals. If you're lucky, you have one or two of these people on your team, and if you spot the potential, nurture it! Six-lane highway workers are the ones who have made themselves irreplaceable, and when you're busy and stressed and don't have a ton of time for hand-holding, you can count on them to get shit done.

Six-laners are risk-takers; they are happy to take a chance and try something new if they think it will inspire others. They are also ideas people, and that often means the role comes with less praise because when they think of the next big thing for your company it's usually someone else (often a one-laner) who is implementing their idea. Six-lane workers usually check their egos at the door, and that's a very good thing. They assume that their work will speak for itself, so if you are overseeing someone who falls into this category, reward them with promotions or raises or more responsibility. Words of praise are great, but six-laners are the ambitious workers who really want to move up in their careers and take on new challenges and prove their value. Six-lane workers also have the potential to manage larger teams, and the foresight to give direction on roles other than their own.

The most important thing to remember when you are managing a team is that there's a place for everyone. All of these workers belong in your company. A team full of six-laners isn't ideal, because you need those one-lane worker bees who are great at execution and specialists in their area. A company of one-laners isn't ideal either, because you'll lack innovation and risk-taking – every day will hum along as it always has, which isn't great for growth. Your job is to recognise what each person's capabilities are and what should be expected from them, and then find out what their goals are, so you can help them grow accordingly. The important thing to remember is that you will probably need to cater to the worker more than you can expect them to cater to you, because people are who they are, and trying to change them won't serve them, you or the company.

When it's time to let go

No matter how careful and intentional you are about hiring, not every employee is going to work out, and this is especially true at a new or young company that's just beginning to figure out the right team make-up. Firing someone sucks, but it's inevitable. And if you are the leader, it's on you.

At both Monday and The Pilates Class, I have had to let go of employees I may have liked, but for one reason or another it just wasn't the right fit. Of course it's not fun – no one enjoys delivering bad news – but I don't shy away from it because it makes sense to me that if someone isn't thriving, you should help them get on a better path. We never fire people unnecessarily. First we try to figure out what they are good at and if there is a different role they'd be better suited to. Sometimes we try to alter the role to fit the worker. But if we do all these things and it's still not working out, then the right thing to do seems pretty obvious.

The truth is, it's rare that an employee loves their job and is happy in a position and feels fulfilled and is suddenly surprised to be let go. That might happen in the movies, but in real life if someone is underperforming or struggling, they usually know it and they don't enjoy it. To me, the reasonable thing to do is say to that person, 'You need to find what makes you happy and where you can shine because this is not it.'

At Monday, for example, we work hard to foster a positive and inspiring work culture. When we have employees who are not aligned with that intention – if they are super negative or not helpful to their co-workers or they love to gossip – we let them go. It's necessary in order to maintain our work environment but also so that the employee can find a job where (a) they are more aligned with the culture or (b) they are happier, and thus less inclined to be negative.

The good news is, you'll probably be able to tell fairly quickly if someone isn't a fit, so have confidence in your intuition. And again, while no one *enjoys* firing people, if someone isn't the right fit for your company, it's not just bad for you, it's bad for them. That's why I don't feel guilty when I let someone go. Not because I'm unfeeling, but because I know that in the long run I am doing them a favour, even if it doesn't feel like it in the moment, and I'm helping protect the company and the team we're building, which always takes top priority.

5

The beauty of starting small

*There's nothing wrong with staying small. You can do
big things with a small team.*

JASON FRIED

These days, people increasingly believe that bigger equals
better. Bigger headcount, bigger following, bigger marketing budget, bigger production value. For some entrepreneurs,
the long-term goal of starting a small business is to eventually grow it into a big business. It makes sense – as you make
more money and your product is more in demand, you'll
need to grow your team and eventually you may want to
expand your offerings. Growth begets growth. But the truth
is, there's so much about being a small business that I prefer.
Smaller companies are agile. They can pivot quickly and be
more experimental. As my companies continue to grow, I do
everything I can to hold on to the small-business mentality
because, frankly, they're just more fun.

The definition of a small business varies between industries
and even between countries. The UK government considers
a business 'small' if it has fewer than fifty employees and

total sales of less than or equal to €10 million annually. In the US, the Small Business Administration defines a small business as having fewer than five hundred employees, but the 'size standards' (the largest your business can be to still get benefits reserved for small businesses) change based on industry. The Australian Tax Office considers any business with an annual turnover of less than AU$10 million to be a small business. No matter what guidelines you use, number of employees and yearly revenue are usually the two defining factors. Technically, both Monday and The Pilates Class are still small, but even as we grow – from very small to a little less small – I focus on maintaining our small-business ethos. You can hope and pray for monster growth, but at some point it can feel like the business has become just that: a monster. You're answering to a board, usually a bunch of men in suits, and it becomes a lot harder to take risks and maintain the work culture you worked so hard to establish.

We're all in this together

The very best thing about being a small business is that, as the founder, you can stay connected to all aspects of the operations, and to all members of the team. And it really does feel like a *team* when a company is still small, not a dictatorship. This can get lost as a company grows. A manager I hired once suggested I send out an org chart – basically a flow chart that indicated who reported to whom, and where everyone fell on the company food chain – and I was quick to say that we have never created a visual hierarchy at Monday, because we don't want anyone to feel like they are below anyone else. In big companies, it can be helpful to understand how different departments are structured and where everyone falls in relation to everyone else, but in smaller organisations that matters far less. Yes, there is a certain chain of command, and people need to know who their direct boss is, but I didn't like the idea of putting something on paper that seemed to indicate a pecking order or assign one person more value than another. When you have a small business, you never know who's going to contribute the next great idea, and you want everyone to feel like their input matters. The worst thing you could do is make someone feel so unimportant that they keep their great ideas to themselves or, even worse, save them for a different company.

As the manager of a small team, your goal should be to have a relationship with every single person on the payroll. You may not be super tight, but you know their name, you have had a conversation, and hopefully they aren't scared of or intimidated by you. (If they are, maybe reconsider your approach – as leader, shoot for a we're-all-in-this-together vibe not a how-dare-you-speak-to-me one.) That's the kind of culture necessary to really inspire your team and infuse in them the same passion for the brand that you have, which is critical when your team is still small but mighty. Dedication to the company needs to trickle down from the top. As companies grow and get more corporate, that level of connection and inspiring leadership can get lost. The minute you start bringing in corporate types who are entirely focused on the numbers and not as in tune with the heart and soul of the brand, you risk losing the very culture that connected and inspired your team to begin with.

Here's the other thing about investors and venture capitalists and the folks who make careers out of taking bets on companies: they usually aren't entrepreneurs themselves, and there's a reason for that. No shade to financers – they are an important part of the business ecosystem, and I know that plenty of businesses stay afloat or grow thanks to their help. But the job of an investor is to mitigate risk, because they don't want to lose their money. I've been on calls with VCs and boardroom types, and they are very good at offering lots of reasons why something can't work. As we know, being an entrepreneur requires taking chances and being creative and going with your gut every once in a while, even if the data tells you otherwise. I enjoy being on those VC calls and building those relationships because I have a lot to learn from people who've worked with different businesses and have been behind the scenes of various success stories. But sometimes as a business owner you need to roll with your intuition, and that's just not an investor's strong suit. And, as a company gets bigger, the ability to rely on intuition gets smaller – either because there is more data available or there's too much at stake or there are more board members breathing down your neck.

There's also a fairly common scenario in which a company is bought out and handed over to a large investment firm, and suddenly the quality of the product or service noticeably declines. It's as if the heart and soul of the brand has disappeared. This is usually because, once sold, the company doesn't have that individual who cares deeply about the brand and maintaining its integrity. Ever wondered why the service at your favourite restaurant or hotel has gone downhill? Or why your favourite clothing brand just doesn't fit or feel the same any more? Look into whether those businesses have changed hands and you'll probably find that they have. This is why some investors choose to keep the previous owners or team members on even after a sale.

Finally, retaining your small business vibe and keeping the team camaraderie intact is simply more fun. No matter how much you grow, you'll want to maintain that piece. Just because you're going to be working your ass off doesn't mean you should be miserable.

Do one thing and do it well

As I've already mentioned, as a business owner you never want to do too much too soon. In the early brainstorming days, it's so easy to get big ideas of how your company could grow. If you start out making eyeglasses, you can eventually expand into contacts and sunglasses. And once you've got sunglasses, what about beach bags? And towels! Or, maybe you offer a subscription food service. After a while, you can start selling your own brand of spices. Or kitchen knives! The possibilities are endless.

It's easy to find yourself just plain giddy at all the opportunities that your original idea affords. But here's my advice: start small. Choose one collection, or one service, and get really good at that one thing. Stick with that one thing for as long as you can. This will allow you to develop your core offering – the product that defines your brand and that will keep people coming back for more. It will also challenge you to find new ways to promote the same product, which is good training for the future, because whether you expand or not, you'll always need to market your core products.

If you find success with your one thing, you will expand eventually. It's inevitable. But, first of all, expansion costs money. If you're continually bringing in new business and retaining previous customers with your first product or service, you can save a lot of money by doing what you've always done and doing it really freaking well. Secondly, adding products or services to your list of offerings requires additional marketing. You've already trained your customers to expect certain things from you – if you add to that, you'll need to invest time and energy into explaining this new product or service to your customer, and why they should buy it from you. There's nothing wrong with all that, but it's additional work (and again, cost), so you want to wait until you have the time and energy to spare. Hopefully, by the time you start expanding, your company is producing that first offering on autopilot. It's a well-oiled machine, so you have employees with time and resources for trying something new.

I know what you're thinking: *Isn't the way to scale a business to start with one product, or in one market, and then slowly add more products, in different categories and markets? Shouldn't I be aiming for growth?* Yes, of course. But I promise, there is no rush. Constantly launching something new or expanding into a new market will put you on a hamster wheel, with no time to enjoy the glory of having conquered your first launch or operating at a steady, reasonable pace. I know many small business owners who let the excitement of creating new products get the better of them, ordering more and more before they've sold through the product they already have. Your initial product, design or service will always be new to new customers, even if it feels old to you.

You want to take this same approach to developing your core audience. I've seen business owners try to launch a service that's targeted to a very wide audience rather than a specific one because they thought that afforded them a higher chance of success. But it's very, very hard to be everything to everyone, especially when you are in the beginning phases of your business. When we launched The Birthing Class, Jacqui and I could have created a platform for women in the pre-conception, pregnancy, birth, postnatal and parenting stages, but we chose to focus on one very important stage and do it right. There's room for expansion but not until it's absolutely necessary and there's no more potential growth within our specific category. Keep in mind, the more specific your target audience, the easier and cheaper your product or service will be to market. So the priority in the beginning should be building a loyal customer base. Then you can slowly expand your offering in a calculated and well-marketed way over time. Start narrow and then widen as needed, but trust me, things fall apart if you overload your team. Focus on expanding smartly, not just quickly.

You might say I learned this lesson the hard way. In 2016, Devin and I decided to launch a line of activewear under the Monday brand. We both lead very active lifestyles, and we wear athleisure and activewear whenever we aren't in swim – if we aren't in bikinis, we're in leggings and sports bras. Good luck finding us in the middle of the day in a pair of jeans. It made sense for us to expand in that direction, and so we debuted Monday Active: thoughtfully designed exercise clothes that we believed in and could actually work out in, and our customers loved it. As a company, we put so much time and effort into that line and we knew it could have been huge, but at the same time, we had so much still to do with swimwear. Monday was a young company, only two years old, and we didn't want to get ahead of ourselves. All the time you spend focusing on your next big thing is time you aren't spending on your bread and butter, and we worried that we were adding in a category we just weren't ready for yet. Every additional category requires new designers, new photo shoots, new manufacturers – it's no small undertaking! It's important to be realistic about how much your company can take on as a brand and a team, and we simply did not have enough people or enough time to focus on creating and promoting great activewear if we also wanted to keep growing and perfecting swim. And one thing I am absolutely sure of is that I want to do something well or not do it at all.

So, despite the fact that we loved Monday Active and our customers *really* loved it, we closed down that category soon after its launch and made a plan to revisit it in the future. It was a bit of a false start, but these things happen. Experimentation is key, and you have to be willing to kill things if they aren't working, or if the time is just not right. That's not a failure, it's a lesson. And the lesson we learned in that moment was that at the right time, activewear would be a natural expansion for us. Seven years later, we had grown our team and our budget, which means we had the capacity to bring Monday Active back, renamed as Monday Body. Now we can do it better than ever, but back then it was a good reminder that there should be no rush to expand. You have to be honest with yourself about what will move the needle and when, and what, in any given moment, is a waste of time and resources. Start small, stay small and expand in increments.

Grow for longevity

Starting small, believe it or not, really is about playing the long game. In any endeavour, having a strong foundation is critical if you want to build something that lasts for ever. It's true of building a house or strengthening your body, and creating a business is no different. That's why I'm so adamantly against chasing quick money or running at a loss. The questions I'm constantly asking myself are: 'Does this thing have legs?' and 'What does twenty years of this brand look like?' I may rely on social media for marketing because, let's face it, that's where most of it's happening these days, but I'm always thinking of how we can exist outside of those platforms because every hot new app eventually becomes old news, and if a business is only successful because it has great Instagram or TikTok content – if the actual product isn't any good, if the customers aren't loyal – than it doesn't really have legs. Starting small is about building that foundation slowly, so it can sustain decades of change.

One reason that many companies would rather cast a wide net than start small, or choose to go for aggressive growth instead of slow and steady, is that they are trying to live up to the competitors around them. They find companies that do similar work or sell in a similar space, and they get caught up in what that business is doing, rather than staying focused on their own. There's a saying that comparison is the thief of joy and I think that's absolutely true, but it's also the thief of growth, and creativity, and success. It's the thief of longevity too, because it's quite hard to stay afloat for a long time if you're modelling your business entirely on someone else's. You'll either always come in second to them, or go down when they do.

It's important to remember that there's enough room in every industry for multiple companies. Yes, you absolutely need to do market research before you start a company. It's imperative that you know who else is doing anything similar to what you want to do, both so you can be sure not to create a product or service that already exists, and so that you can be clear on your points of difference and can speak to those distinctions with authority. You don't need to compare and compete as if only the strongest will survive, because you can coexist. And hopefully your product is different enough that you are not *directly* competing with anyone – you should be able to explain, quickly and succinctly, how you are different from every other offering in the market. When I first started Monday, I was often tempted to look at what other swim companies were doing, but I always found it counterproductive and damaging to my own creative flow. It either made me question my own work or wonder if we should pursue something that deep down I knew wasn't my passion. I had to keep my focus on what mattered: designs that catered to the Monday customer's needs. So rather than getting caught up in the race for growth because you envy other companies in your industry, or you want to be as big or flashy as them, focus inwards. Get OK with the fact that you may not be as big as the competitors just yet. You probably won't be for a while, and that's just fine. The truth is, I've always loved being a small fish in a big pond. I get claustrophobic in spaces where there is no room to grow and mature. I'm much happier in a world of opportunity, and maintaining that small-business mentality means there is always a new opportunity – you aren't blowing all your chances at new things right out of the gate.

Never mind the copycats

Just as you don't want to get sidetracked by comparing yourself to other companies or competing with them, I would similarly caution you against getting worked up by others who copy *you*. At Monday, we have been blatantly imitated by other brands more times than I can count. We've even seen business owners order a product under their own name, and then clearly try to recreate the item they bought at their own company. But we make a choice not to get caught up or worry about the competition because if you always stay ahead of the game, people can copy all they want. I know some business owners who have spent thousands of dollars hiring lawyers to chase after people who have copied their products, ultimately driving their business into the ground because of the legal fees, when they really should have invested that money into the growth of their brand. Owners of small brands get so disheartened when the giant corporations take what they've spent time and money creating and recreate it with the slightest modifications and call it their own. I understand. Is it fair that people do this? No. But it's the way of the world and something you ought to get used to sooner rather than later. Sometimes a legal battle *is* justified, especially if you have a patent, but I've never wasted time being upset about a copycat. It's just another reason why you need to remain inventive, and make your service or product better than the rest!

One last note about small, independently owned businesses: there's a reason why people love them. Why consumers believe in and brag about supporting them, and why there are endless initiatives to remind people to buy from them. It's because there really is a beauty to the idea that these businesses are someone's passion, that there are human beings and intention behind every product and purchase. Consumers can feel that authenticity, so don't lose sight of it. Because as much as your loyal following will appreciate the authenticity of your brand, they can just as easily sniff it out when that goes away.

6

Finances, data, logistics, oh my!

The greatest bit of advice I ever received was, 'Don't worry, no one else knows what they're doing either.'

RICKY GERVAIS

When Devin and I started Monday, the biggest mystery to us was one seemingly simple but entirely critical question: 'How do we *become* a business?' Let's say you have an idea, and you have friends who have signed up to help you create your product or build your service. How do you go from a person selling something out of their living room to a verified small business, with all the paperwork and legal protections that entails?

For most of us who didn't get a business degree, these practical steps are the real black box. It's not just the *how* to do it that's hard, but even figuring out *what* you need to do. It's daunting, and it's often the barrier to entry that keeps plenty of great ideas from becoming real businesses. I've heard 'I don't even know where to start' from too many aspiring entrepreneurs who otherwise have all the potential for success.

I figured most of it out as I went along, asking questions of anyone and everyone I could, and googling the rest. The answers are out there, as long as you're willing to put in the time poring over search results, but I want to save you the energy and offer you an understanding of what to do and where to start, because if you really are excessively obsessed with your concept, the confusion over how to register a business shouldn't be what keeps you away.

What's in a name?

One of the very first decisions you'll have to make when you venture into entrepreneurism is what to name your business. You want to get this right from the beginning. Yes, you can change your company name later, and plenty of companies do, but it's not particularly easy. It involves rebranding to attract new customers while also working hard to retain your existing customers – an added headache you're better off avoiding – so the goal should be to pick a name that can stick with you as you grow.

Devin and I used to always joke that, 'If you're in a bikini on a Monday, you're having a good day', and that's ultimately how we came up with our brand name. We wanted to create swimsuits that made women feel good – like they were having a great day just by wearing them – and to this day that's our driving goal. In moments when we have to make decisions about whether to add to a line or expand into a new category, this is what we come back to: can we do this new thing while still honouring our original intention as a business? Sometimes the answer is yes and sometimes it's no, but this understanding of who we are, and who we started out as, helps us figure out what's right for us and for our loyal customers.

As you are thinking through potential names for your business, it's important to keep in mind that you want to choose something short and memorable, or that describes (or at least hints at) what your product or service is. Monday is maybe not obviously swimwear, but when we first started the business, every single one of our hangtags said, 'If you're wearing a bikini on a Monday, it's a good day!' With those twelve words, the connection was clear and our customers got it. The name was a little bit cheeky but also deliberate: here was a product intended for moments of indulgence and living your most fabulous life.

When we named The Pilates Class (and later The Birthing Class), we went the 'direct and obvious' route. What we do is right there in the name. And sure, over time we've grown and expanded into HIIT classes and barre and stretching, but they all incorporate Pilates, because that's our core business. An ambiguous name can be just as successful, but in a world where SEO (search engine optimisation, more on that on page 180) and getting your brand out there can be costly, it can be easier to use your name as a marketing tool in itself.

If choosing your company name is the first big decision, creating a slogan might come next. Business slogans help give context to your name, especially if you go with one that's not entirely clear. Because they are longer, slogans offer opportunities for explanation, and since they aren't your registered name, they are far easier to change as your company changes. Consider Amazon. When the company started, its slogan was 'Earth's biggest bookstore.' Today, that slogan feels completely unrelated to what the company has become. These days, it has multiple slogans, including 'Work Hard. Have Fun. Make History.'

The name game

Naming a company is hard. Think of any brand name that seems obvious or simple to you as an outsider ... I can guarantee you a team of people spent hours poring over options and deliberating about what was best. Here are some best practices to keep in mind as you play the name game. You don't have to check off every item, but the more the better.

- **Can it expand?** If your brand name is very specific to the exact product you produce or service you offer, it can be complicated if and when you decide to expand. Try to pick a name that can grow with your company.
- **Does it stand out?** You don't want a name that's so similar to your competitors that people can't distinguish or remember who you are.
- **Does it open you up to legal action?** Make sure you are checking for trademarks, and you don't pick a name that is too similar to another company.
- **Can people pronounce it?** Don't try so hard to use a clever spelling that people can't figure out how to say (or spell) your company name.
- **Does it evoke the right emotion?** This one is probably the most subjective but you probably don't want to choose a term that sounds very technical if yours is a whimsical fabric company. Similarly, you may not want to go with too silly a word if you are offering, say, a medical-related service.

Getting started: a checklist

Now that you've got your name, you're ready to establish your business. Here's a list of questions to ask yourself to get the ball rolling ...

Is the name available?

There are lots of businesses out there, and it's entirely possible that the name you've chosen is already claimed. You can find this out (free of charge) by searching the UK or US trademark databases online, as well as in any other countries that are relevant markets for your business. If the name *is* available, you'll need a trademark in order to claim it, and you'll want to register that trademark under every category your company might venture into. (But don't go crazy – you need to have a good-faith intent to use the trademark on all the goods and services you apply under.) For example, Monday has a trademark for a number of goods and services: footwear, headwear, lingerie, sweaters, swimwear, underwear, towels, beach towels, sunglasses and sunglasses/eyeglasses cases. We wouldn't just apply for a trademark for fishing rods, because it's unlikely we'd use it, but it's reasonable to assume we might design beach towels, so we got ahead of that.

Are the URLs available?

If you have a great original name for your business but you can't get the URL for it, or for a name quite similar, you might want to rethink the name entirely. No matter what your business, you need an online presence, and your website name should be intuitive for your customers. If they can't find you, they can't buy anything from you. (You might want to check that social media handles – with the name or something very close – are available as well.) As with your trademark, consider every country where you expect to do business – you will want a .com domain, but you may also want to own the rights to .co.uk for the UK and .com.au for Australia, and so on. You should also consider buying any URLs that are similar to your name. For example, the domain for Monday is mondayswimwear.com, but we also bought mondayswim.com, and if you go there by mistake, you'll be redirected to our site. You want to make it as easy as possible for potential customers to find you. You can obtain a domain name/URL through multiple different sites – just google it. Domain names are relatively cheap, but some people make a business out of pre-purchasing URLs to sell at a higher price to someone who wants them later. Still, depending on the price, this should be considered a worthwhile investment.

Do you have an accountant?

The paperwork necessary to launch your business can feel overwhelming and a bit scary, especially the paperwork related to finances and paying taxes and making sure you're in compliance with all the legal requirements of being a company. What's required of you can be confusing, and the consequences of doing something wrong – even if you never intended to – can be serious, at least in terms of getting hit with fines and other unexpected fees. Hiring an accountant who is experienced in working with small businesses is money well spent. It will buy you expertise in the form of a professional who can guide you through the process and make sure you've done everything you need to do and done it correctly, but it will also buy you a little peace of mind. This is where you might want to tap into friends, family and colleagues for recommendations. In the chaos of starting a company, finding a small business accountant you can trust is invaluable.

What is your business structure?

Your business could be a sole proprietorship, a partnership, an LLC (limited liability company) or a corporation (depending on your country). The choice depends on various factors including whether you own the company alone or with a partner, what proportion of your personal assets you want to protect, and whether you plan to take on investors or go public one day. There are benefits to each, but the structure you choose makes a difference: it affects your legal protections, taxes, the paperwork you need to file (and the cost of filing) and your personal financial responsibility if things go wrong. Monday and The Pilates Class both started as LLCs; this structure protects business owners from personal liability if the business goes under or faces a lawsuit. But when you're just starting out, a sole proprietorship or partnership structure might make more sense for you. This is an issue you might want to discuss with your lawyer or accountant, but there are also plenty of resources online to help you decide. Once you have settled on your name and business structure, you need to register your business under that name. For my first company, I went down to the local registration office in person and filed the paperwork myself. It may sound complicated, but it tends to be pretty straightforward once you get started.

Do you have an Employer Reference Number (ERN) or Tax Identification Number (TIN), Unique Tax Reference Number (UTR) or your country's equivalent?

This is the number you will need for tax purposes, similar to your personal National Insurance or Social Security number. It's necessary to pay taxes, open a bank account, hire employees and apply for certain business licences. Applying is free and easy online, but if you have concerns or questions, talk to your accountant.

Do you have a bank account?

If you want to spend money as a business – or, more importantly, *get* money as a business – you need a business bank account. It could be a current account or savings account or, if you are planning to accept credit card transactions from customers, a merchant services account. You can't open it until you have your ERN, but it should be your next step once that reference number is issued. You should be able to do this easily enough by going to your local bank branch, but if you're confused about what makes the most sense for your business, this is another question for your accountant. (I told you this would be an important asset!)

Where is your market?

Will you launch globally, or only in one country? And if you are based in one country, will you ship internationally? Generally, I would suggest starting with a more local customer base and then expanding as necessary, but that's not always possible. Social media is a global space, and sometimes the decision as to who your audience will be isn't in your hands, especially if the demand for your product is global early on (good problem to have, I know). If you are based in one country and need to ship internationally, there are different taxes associated and sometimes very high shipping costs, so be sure you understand the implications of shipping overseas if that's relevant. Or decide early on that you won't ship overseas to start, and be clear about that in your marketing materials.

Do you need a lawyer?

You don't necessarily need a lawyer – a lawyer is less important than an accountant, I would say – but a good corporate lawyer can be a huge help and can lead you through some of the processes I've already mentioned, like getting a trademark. A lawyer might also help you determine if you need a patent for your product or what type of business structure makes the most sense for your particular company, and may help to review contracts. And if you are entering into any sort of partnership, I definitely recommend working with a lawyer on this agreement. As is the case with an accountant, having a lawyer who is well versed in business when you are relatively new can provide a level of comfort that may pay for itself.

Understanding margins

There are some terms and concepts that, if you are going to sell a good or service for money, you will want to understand. A bunch of them you will learn as you go, and that's fine, it's part of the journey. But others you are better off knowing at the outset, both so you can have an informed conversation about your business and so you can understand what's necessary to set yourself up for financial success. Understanding margins – a good indicator of how much money your business is making or has the potential to make – is one thing that really shouldn't wait for later. This is something you want to know now.

Profit margins represent the difference between the amount of money your business brings in and the cost to your company of doing business. The higher the margins, the more money your business is making.

There two different types of profit margin you will want to consider when you first start out: gross and net.

Gross margins

Your gross margin is calculated by taking the sale price of your product and subtracting the costs associated with making the product (also known as the costs of goods sold, or COGS). This will include, for example, the cost of fabric if you are making a piece of clothing but also the cost of shipping and packaging that piece of clothing, and any direct labour you need to pay for. COGS doesn't include any of your business's general operating expenses, like marketing or payroll or office rent, it's just about the amount you directly spend to produce a product. So, if your company makes a sweater that costs you $80 – that's the combined cost of buying the material and paying to have the sweater made in a factory and then shipped to you – and you sell it for $100, your margin on that sweater is $20, or 20 per cent. When people talk about gross margins, they talk in percentages, and the percentage is determined by taking the difference between your sales price and COGS, and dividing that number by sales price. (So, in the example above, the difference between the sale price and the COGS is $20. You divide that number by the sales price, $100, and you get .20, or 20 per cent.)

Calculating gross margin

Gross profit = Selling price – Cost price
Gross profit = $100 – $80 = $20
Gross margin = (Profit / Sales price) × 100%
Gross margin % = ($20 / $100) × 100% = 20%

Understanding your gross margins will help you determine how to price a product, because you want to be sure you are charging enough to make the cost of making the product worth it.

Net margins

Your company's net profit margins represent the money you've made after all your business expenses are accounted for. So rather than only considering the cost of goods sold, or COGS, you are subtracting that *as well as* overheads and operating costs like payroll or office rent, taxes and any additional expenses. As is the case with gross margins, net margins are expressed as a percentage and calculated similarly: take the difference between gross sales and expenses to determine your net income, and divide that number by gross sales.

Your net margin is an important number to know because it represents your company's overall financial health. It gives a more accurate view of the company's profitability, because you may have high gross margins, but if you are overspending on things like office rent or have more employees than you can afford, your net profit can still be quite low.

*

For both margins, in general, 5 per cent is considered low, 7–10 per cent is healthy, and 30 per cent is high. But a blanket statement like that can be misleading, because different types of businesses have different expected margins. Service businesses, for example, have very high gross margins because their COGS is low, since there is no physical product to create. Apparel generally has high margins as well, because the cost of making the goods is low (this is especially true when you are a small business and you have fewer operating costs). Tech companies, for example, can have margins of 50–90 per cent. Restaurants, on the other hand, typically have low margins because there are such high operating costs. To keep a restaurant up and running you need to pay for rent, equipment, labour, food and beverage costs, and more. According to a 2020 article from *Restaurant Manager* magazine, the average full-service restaurant has a profit margin of only 3–5 per cent.

Understanding profit margins is critical for a number of reasons. Of course, there's the obvious: you want to know how much money you're making, or how much money you stand to make. When you're starting out, having a grasp of these figures will help you determine how much to charge for your product or service. Once you are up and running, knowing your margins will also help you determine how much you can afford to reinvest into the business.

I'll be honest, I knew almost nothing about margins when I started Monday. I just loved swimwear. I was extremely lucky that it turned out to be an industry with great margins. And because we sell our suits direct to consumer rather than wholesale (translation: our customers are buying our suits direct from Monday, rather than from a third-party retail website that sells our products) our margins are even higher, because no one else takes a piece of each sale. Once I realised this, and learned more about margins and what they represent, I knew I would only start or invest in companies with similarly healthy margins. Not because I'm fixated on profit, but because I want to have cash to reinvest in the business – I want to be able to hire a great team, and spend on marketing, and feel secure in our ability to do that. In that regard, The Pilates Class is a dream. We started with low overhead costs, which means our margins are significant and we have plenty of cash to reinvest in growing and improving our business.

Now, I want to be clear about one thing: you can have a successful company with low margins. I'm not saying that I only want to be in high-margin companies because low margins are inherently bad. Like I said, if you are passionate about opening a restaurant, I'd be the first to tell you to do it, low margins and all. But if you are working in an industry or at a company with low margins, you do need to approach the business differently. You will need to pay close attention to every dollar spent, and you aren't going to have as much to spend on development and growth. As a business owner, I like being experimental and spending on business development and growth, and you have to be more conservative on those fronts when you are running a business with smaller margins.

Ordering product

If your company revolves around selling a product, you need to have the product in stock in order to sell it and ship it to customers. Figuring out how much of that product to order is a bit of a dance – you want to have enough to fulfil orders but not so much that you end up with rooms full of unsold inventory (as you'll see in the next chapter, I'm speaking from experience here). This is extra hard when you're starting out.

You're building an audience and you have no previous data to base your estimate on, so maybe you throw a number at the wall and hope it sticks. Maybe you base it on how many followers you have, but not everyone who follows you is actually going to convert to a purchase. A general rule of thumb is that e-commerce sites will, on average, see a 1–4 per cent conversion rate. Let's say you've built up your social following and begun some basic marketing and you have an audience of five thousand people that you've teased your product to, by sharing photos or 'coming soon' posts. (If you're building a storefront business but you're not yet on social, your 'teaser' might instead be local mailbox drops and a sign in the window with a tentative opening date.) And let's pretend that all five thousand of those people actually clicked on your website when you promoted your launch. If we use 2 per cent as a safe conversion rate, that means you will sell one hundred products. But, there's a catch! Not all five thousand people you launch to will actually click on your website. That number will vary based on excitement or demand or the success of your launch (more on how to launch on page 211), but if you got a 10 per cent click rate that would be a really good day. That means you'd get five hundred people to your site (10 per cent of five thousand) and make ten sales (2 per cent of five hundred).

These conversion rates can be really sobering for a young, excited entrepreneur who is planning to order thousands of units of a product that they plan to get rich from, but it's so important to understand because I've seen families, couples, business partners and individuals lose their life savings when buying into a product too aggressively. This is usually because a vendor or manufacturer has a minimum order quantity of, say, three thousand units across all styles or colourways, and an entrepreneur will feel like they have no choice. I strongly suggest taking the slow approach and finding a local vendor that can help you make your product in lower quantities. Yes, sometimes that will mean it's more expensive to make, but it's better than being stuck with three thousand units of a product you can't sell and being even more in the hole.

Now, let's say you do order only five hundred units of your product and you sell them all within the first few months and can't restock fast enough to meet demand. Now you're thinking, *Ugh, that bloody Tash Oakley told me not to order more and I'm screwed!* Take a breath. It's OK. First of all, congratulations! There is demand for your product. Second of all, this is not a disaster. Let your customers know when the product will be back in stock, and build up a wait list or allow pre-orders if it's possible with your business model. In the early stages, especially if you're spending your own money, it's better to start slow and build excitement and demand. Just remember that whoever you get to your site, only an average of 2.5 per cent of them will buy your product – and that's a statistic you cannot cheat.

The psychology of pricing

There's a lot that goes into pricing, whatever it is you are selling. Margins are one part of the equation, for sure, but certainly not the whole thing. At Monday, our prices are based largely on the quality of our suits. But there's also a lot of consumer psychology that needs to be taken into consideration when it comes to choosing the cost of your goods. People have a lot of preconceived notions when it comes to prices. If our suits were much cheaper, for example, customers might think of the product differently, and not order it at all because they'd assume it isn't high quality.

With luxury brands, pricing has less to do with the cost of making the goods or the materials used, and more to do with status. For high-end luxury designers, for example, exclusivity is a cornerstone of their marketing strategy. It's what distinguishes them as a brand, so these businesses can afford to make fewer sales because the margin on their product is so high. For these companies, expenses come more in the form of marketing and the efforts that go into turning their products into status symbols.

For some services, a price is established based on the customer being targeted. At The Pilates Class, we wanted to be able to invest in a premium product for our members – high-quality classes with in-demand instructors – but we also wanted the ability to build out our technology and offerings, which is how we landed on a higher monthly membership fee. We also wanted to attract a customer who invests in a brand they love, because those customers are quite loyal. We could have priced lower to target a wider market, but that might have led some customers to subscribe (or unsubscribe) on impulse, which we felt could weaken our brand loyalty and potential for growth. But that's just what makes sense for us – there is no single pricing model that is better than others. There can be many benefits to pricing something low, since the less something costs the less time a consumer will spend thinking about buying it or investing in it, which might translate to building a larger audience, faster. Mass-market apparel brands charge less, for example, but they make a killing if huge numbers of customers buy what they're selling. There's no one right way to do things overall, but, depending on your business goals, there might be a right way to do things for you.

Budgeting basics

Budgeting for your business is hardest when you're just starting out. When you've had a company for a year, or even six months, you have some data to rely on. You have a sense of how much money your business brings in, and how much you generally spend to operate. But at the beginning, before year one, it's all just conjecture. Informed assumptions. You're guessing, pretty much, though hopefully it's educated guessing. Two factors you will want to consider in those early days are:

- How much do you reasonably hope to make in your first year?
- How much inventory do you need to buy to reach that goal, and how much money do you have to start out with (based on your funds, or loans, or angel investments)?

Worksheet: Budget brainstorm

Figuring out your budget is hard when your business is still a baby. But there are some questions you can ask yourself to help you make informed decisions. Use the space provided here to consider your answers to the following questions, which can help you establish your first-year budget. (For a sample budgeting sheet see Appendix A, page 267.)

How much money do I reasonably hope to make in the first year? How did I come to this number?

_____

_____

_____

_____

_____

_____

_____

How much product do I need to sell to reach my first-year profit goals? How much product should I order in advance to reach those sales goals? Why?

_____

_____

_____

_____

_____

_____

_____

How much money will I start out with, and how much of that can I allocate to ordering product?

_____

_____

_____

_____

_____

_____

_____

What other costs do I need to consider in our first year? Will I be hiring employees? Paying for marketing? Renting office space? List any expected additional costs.

_____

_____

_____

_____

_____

_____

_____

Work with your accountant to ensure the numbers you're envisioning are reasonable, and that you can actually afford whatever budget you've come up with. Then, start slowly – try to build a community and generate interest among potential consumers before you actually launch anything, so that you will already have a customer base the moment your business goes live (more on how to do this in Chapter 10). Time, after all, is money, and the longer your business is up and running without any customers, the more it will cost you.

After you've been in business for about a year, you will be better able to make accurate projections. I always base my budgets on a twelve-month projection. A full year of data really is better than six months, because so much of customer behaviour is seasonal. Of course that's especially true with something like swimsuits, but every business has its own seasonal customer behaviour. Sales might go up at holiday time or around Mother's Day, because your company makes giftable products. Or maybe you see a peak just before the New Year, because you sell a 'self-improvement' service that people seek out when it's time to make resolutions. Every industry has seasonal trends, so you'll want to keep a close eye not just on when your customers buy your product or service but also when they buy your competitors' product or service. If all our competitors are doing their summer sale earlier than Monday, for example, then by the time our sale happens, consumers might already have spent on their swimsuits for the year. In that regard, you want stay on top of market trends and adjust your own business accordingly.

As you are determining how much you can afford to spend on employees, marketing, legal fees and more, keep in mind that your budget should also account for savings. You should always have at least three to six months of operating costs in your savings, no matter what. In some cases – if your margins are low or cash flow is tight – you'll want even more.

If you're reading these paragraphs and your eyes are starting to cross, I get it. In school I despised mathematics, but these days I'm pretty great with data and numbers and analysis. When the numbers refer to your own business, something you are literally and figuratively invested in – in terms of your money but also in terms your heart and soul – they suddenly feel a lot more interesting and important. And in the very beginning stages, your budget might be quite straightforward anyway. When I was twenty-one and we started Monday, for example, I didn't create a goal – we just kept every cost down, worked as hard as we could and banked up savings from the money coming in. Our Excel budget spreadsheet might have had fifteen to twenty lines, now it has 250. And at this point, I don't want to be the one managing payroll or taxes or crunching numbers for my company. If finance is your thing, kudos to you. But if it's not, you're not alone, and this is why you need to find people you trust to assist you with budgets and projections and actuals. You don't want to push your business off track due to any huge financial errors, and while I've talked about taking risks, it seems relevant to reiterate here that all risks should be calculated – monetary risks especially. That's why I've always been happy to take our growth a little slower and play things a little safer. Running a profitable company as soon as possible has always been a priority.

User-friendly business tools

Here's a list of easy-to-use and relatively affordable programs that I utilise within my businesses (at the time of writing this book) to streamline our operations and logistics. I've listed them in the order that I chose to implement them into my company, so that you too can start from the top and work your way down. There are several good options in each category that you can research on your own – those I've listed aren't necessarily the gold standard, they're just what worked for me. As a business owner, it's your duty to stay on top of tech updates, and to implement new systems and programs over time.

- **Shopify:** At Monday, we have always used the e-commerce platform Shopify to host our online store. Its sales reporting is extremely useful for planning and analysing all aspects of the business.
- **Zendesk:** This easy-to-use customer service platform allows multiple team members to simultaneously answer and organise enquiries.
- **Google Docs, Sheets, Drive and Calendar:** At all my companies, we use Google for all of our documents because it allows team members to synchronously collaborate on documents. Google Calendar is universal and very useful in maintaining your business meeting calendar.
- **QuickBooks:** This accounting software helps business owners easily manage company finances. Reports and breakdowns help you stay on top of both incoming revenue and outgoing expenses.
- **Mailchimp or Klaviyo:** These platforms offer email marketing, including automation, for even the smallest of brands.

- **Planoly:** A social media planner you can use to schedule posts, organise content or manage multiple accounts in one place.
- **Slack:** Messaging service that allows you to organise your teams' communication into project-, department- or topic-specific channels.
- **Loop Returns:** Loop's straightforward systems help brands that use Shopify optimise return costs, retain more revenue and prevent return losses.
- **Attentive:** User-friendly SMS marketing platform.
- **Dropbox:** Storage for online documents and images that you can easily share with others.
- **Canva:** Online graphic design tool.
- **Zoom, Google Meet or Teams:** Online meeting hosts.

Data is a guide, not a dictator

Companies have more data about their customers today than ever before. The variety and depth of data that a company can gather could fill a book of its own (and plenty of those books exist!), but at a high level, most small businesses are gathering data on customer demographics, sales, repeat customers, returns, and much more, using analytics platforms like Shopify. The information that data provides is invaluable – it can help you understand who your customer is and how they shop, find out if a product isn't working and change course, and understand what your customer wants more of and innovate accordingly. But data is only one piece of the business puzzle, and you can't follow it blindly.

Knowing when to rely on data and when to rely on your own intuition and creativity can be tricky. It's hard to trust yourself if the numbers tell you something different. But, in my experience, not all data is created equal. Sometimes you have to accept that the numbers don't lie, and you should follow the data whether you like it or not. But sometimes you have to embrace a level of risk and inventiveness in order to grow and expand and make your mark on your company. And sometimes you need to find a happy balance of the two.

For me and my businesses, the most important data will always be sales data: what is selling well and what is not. At Monday, we might be selling a one-piece that I am absolutely in love with, that I think is gorgeous and will fly off the (virtual) shelves. Then I might look at the data and see that the one-piece is selling just OK, but there's this little red bikini top that we can't seem to keep in stock. It may not be my personal go-to, but it doesn't matter, we have to follow the sales trend and order more of the bikini top and fewer of the one-piece. If you're starting a product-based company, eventually you'll hire someone who manages your inventory and writes your orders, but in your earliest business days, that will most likely be you, so you have to follow the data and not get emotionally attached to any one product. The data will tell you where you need more inventory, no matter how much you might love your equivalent of my adorable little one-piece. What you think is good might differ from what the customer is buying, and that is information no business owner can ignore. It is what will turn your creative project into a commercial brand.

This holds true even if you aren't selling a physical product, of course. At The Pilates Class, we offer all different lengths of classes. If I notice that our twenty-minute sessions are the most popular, I need to offer more of them, even if

I personally prefer a forty-five-minute workout. Customers speak with their wallets and their clicks, so if they're investing money or time into a specific product, we want to be sure we have it available.

There are some categories of data that are important and insightful, and should inform some decisions, but need to be taken in context. Consider demographic data. Sure, it's important to have a full picture of your typical customer – age range, where they live, their typical income, that sort of thing. But if you cater exclusively to who your customers have been in the past, you miss an opportunity to bring in a new and more diverse customer base in the future.

In the earliest days of your business in particular, your demographic data might hold a lot of weight, especially because sometimes the person that resonates most with your product isn't who you thought it would be. If you understand who you are talking to, what they like buying, their purchasing behaviour, if they live in a big city or small town – all of that can inform your branding and marketing messaging. You can tailor your content to that person so they keep coming back and so that you attract more, similar customers who you're confident will like your product. Having a sense of your typical customer can dictate how you write online copy, where you devote your advertising spend, and more. But as important as it is to know who your *current* customer is, it's equally important to remember that there's potential for anyone to be your *future* customer. If you get too narrow-minded in your approach, you can shut out or deter wide swathes of people who might otherwise be eager to spend their money with your business. You never know what unexpected group may resonate with your brand.

You also have to keep in mind your company's values. Encouraging diversity and instilling body confidence in all women is a core value of ours at all of my brands. At Monday, we have a wide range of sizes in our models and our offerings. If we were going to listen to the data, we would offer only two or three sizes. Small and medium are our bestsellers, so we could make an argument for selling only those two, or only selling small, medium and large. But that's not who we are or what we believe in, so we sell seven sizes – from petite to very very voluptuous, because we want to include and appeal to a wider range of women.

Finally, we have some categories of data that, sure, I'll gather and take a look at, but I generally don't let it drive decisions. When we collect market data or customer surveys, we usually ask the customer what they want – what's something they want to see more of, or something we haven't done that they wish we did. Or we might be even more direct. We might say, which do you like better, purple or blue? And they might say blue, but the truth is, the customer doesn't always know what they want. Or they think they want one thing – a blue suit – but then you launch a purple you really believe in and do a great job marketing it and they buy it regardless. At the end of the day you have to trust your intuition, and know that you have some control in helping to persuade people of what they want.

It could also be true that what you're thinking of doing is so innovative that your customer wouldn't even know to request it! There's a quote I love, which is often attributed to Henry Ford – it's one I always think of when we do these customer surveys: 'If I had asked people what they wanted, they would have said "a faster horse".' It was true then, and it's true now.

In general, it's important to collect as much data as possible related to your business because information is power, but you can't live and die by the numbers. Hopefully, you started whatever business you did because you have big ideas. Don't let the numbers take away from your creativity, and trust your passion – after all, it got you this far!

Time management

When you are building a business, there's a lot to do, and only a finite amount of time in which to do it. I don't believe in the idea that you can't ever take a break – working 24/7 is neither sustainable nor healthy. If there's one saying I live by, it's 'work smarter, not harder'. After all, this is the only way you'll ever achieve the coveted four-hour working week, and you can get a lot done in less time if you're smart about it. Thoughtful time-management strategies make it easier to direct your energy and dedicate more hours to the highest-priority areas of your business. Here are a few that I follow myself, and some that I implement with my teams:

- **Organise your to-do list by priority.** My list has tasks for today, this week, this month and this year, as well as an area for those that are urgent.
- **Delegate any tasks that can be handled by other team members.** There are certain parts of my businesses that only I can drive, so I try to stay in my lane and hand off anything else to members of my team. When Jacqui and I brought on new team members to TPC, we did so in part because she was spreading herself too thin. I suggested that she adopt my approach and focus on the roles that only she can play – being the face of the brand, hosting events, filming classes, working on fitness strategy for the brand. Once she'd delegated the work that others

could do for her, she was able to focus entirely on being the face of the brand – she was happier, and so was the team.

- **Audit your time.** If you or a team member feel like you can never get ahead of your workload, document a task-by-task and hour-by-hour diary of what you do in a one- or two-week period. At the end of the designated period, take a look at which areas are getting most of your time. Are there roles or tasks that are consuming your attention that could be deprioritised or delegated to another team member? Some digital platforms (like Monday.com – no relation to my company!) can help with this.

- **Set weekly or monthly meetings to go over agendas.** This will help the team stay organised and create a forum to discuss strategy within a structured environment (rather than a free-for-all that goes on for ever). Take notes in all of these meetings and add any action items to to-do lists, listed in order of priority.

- **Set meeting times, and stick to them.** When the creative juices are flowing, it can be easy to get off track and brainstorm for hours. I have absolutely been guilty of this! Try to stick to the beginning and end times of all your meetings, so your other work does not fall behind.

- **Learn to say no.** If you are in a management or leadership role, team members may come to you for advice or to ask for help with matters they probably could have handled themselves if you weren't available to them. This is especially true if you work together in an office environment. Close your door, block off work hours on your schedule, or get comfortable saying that you aren't available for consultation right now.

- **Implement programs like Slack.** These kinds of organised communication platforms help categorise conversations into different subjects, projects and even search tags. Streamlining internal communication in this manner helps avoids hundred-message-long email chains, which can be a surprisingly big time suck.

- **Discourage unannounced 'pop-ins'.** If you are working in an office environment, encourage your team to 'Slack' or email one another to check whether they have a moment to chat or meet if it wasn't previously scheduled. That way workflows won't constantly be interrupted by someone popping over with a 'quick question'.

- **Keep low-priority meetings remote.** I'm a big fan of face-to-face meetings, but I'm selective about which ones I add to my calendar. Commuting to meetings can eat up your time, and in-person meetings generally run longer than those over Zoom. Even meetings with overseas manufacturers that previously needed to happen in person can now take place remotely.

- **Use artificial intelligence.** It's the way of the future, whether you like it or not, and there are so many ways you can utilise AI to streamline your operations. We use platforms like ChatGPT for copywriting and research, and we're even looking at reducing the workload of our accounting teams by having AI do month-to-month comparisons of our finances. The ways you use AI will depend on the industry you're in, but there are endless options and the sooner you implement them the better!

The stages of growth

Once you've launched your company and are focused on scaling, remember that growth is never perfectly linear. Many businesses have rapid growth out of the gate, but then struggle to grow even 5 per cent year over year (YoY). It makes sense – when you start from nothing, you can only go up from there. When you're established and have secured your loyal customer base, it's harder to build on that. You're already big, so there's not necessarily a lot of room to grow. At Monday, we grew at a 100 per cent growth rate YoY for the first six years – this was quite unusual and is not at all something to rely on. These days we grow at a rate of 30 per cent per year, and we still feel quite lucky. But it's a double-edged sword: aggressive growth can be extremely debilitating for a new company because, yes, you need additional inventory to cover the sales, but you also need to be able to handle increased customer service enquiries, shipping and logistics issues, and potentially hiring additional team members.

If you do achieve steady growth at a healthy rate for the business, your role will be ever changing. I remember at least ten different times that I felt Monday was operating like a well-oiled machine and then just a few months later we'd have new requirements or considerations due to our growth and I'd have to step back in to lead in a more hands-on fashion. I am still growing and evolving as the CEO of my companies, and hopefully always will be.

I think of Monday and The Pilates Class as in their growth phase, while The Birthing Class is still in the start-up phase. The traditional growth stages of a business are: start-up, growth, maturity, renewal or decline. Let's look at Victoria's Secret, a company that has been through many iterations. It had its start-up phase when founder Roy Raymond opened the company in California in 1977. The business was doing $4 million in revenue, but it wasn't making a profit and was bordering on bankruptcy. In 1982, it was purchased by L Brands, a retail holding company, which transitioned Victoria's Secret into a serious growth phase. By the early 1990s, it was the largest lingerie retailer in the US, with 350 stores and $1 billion in sales. This growth continued for a long time, with Sharen Jester Turney becoming overall CEO in 2006 and leading the company to 70 per cent sales growth amounting to $7.7 billion. Between 2015 and 2018, Victoria's Secret entered its maturity phase, as more body-positive brands like Aerie took a part of its market share. Victoria's Secret went from having a 33 per cent to 24 per cent market share. The brand went through a turbulent period due to its complete lack of diversity, both inside the company and out. It refused to change with the times, and when Covid hit it was the final gut punch, forcing the company to close as many as 250 stores. Left with no real choice, it finally made the changes its customers had been calling for and attempted a renewal of the business, which was well into its decline phase. This is not only the perfect illustration of the different stages of growth a business will go through but also a critical reminder of how important it is to evolve as a business. Your marketing strategy is so important, and if you are out of touch with the world around you, your customer can immobilise your business, no matter how big or small. But every business is subject to this cycle – and sometimes it can happen over a matter of years rather than decades, especially for a business that capitalises on a fad or that grows too quickly. This is why slow and steady wins the race. Go for organic growth, build a strong foundation for your business and keep your finger on the pulse – or else!

What's your end goal?

As you are getting the brass tacks of your business in order, especially your financial plans, it's worth considering what your ultimate end goal for your business might be. Do you want to just be the founder and/or CEO, and help your business grow and thrive for as long as you can? That's a great option. Maybe your hope is to launch and build the business, and have enough success that you can eventually sell to a bigger company. And if that's the goal, the next question might be, would you then want to work at that big company? Or use the sale as an exit package? You may even hope to be creating a business that can go public one day. These are all long-term goals, and they certainly aren't set in stone. You might go in with one goal and then, later, reconsider. I launched The Pilates Class thinking it was something that perhaps we would sell in five years, but now I believe we have so much growth opportunity and so much more still to do that I don't feel that way any more (and I can't imagine my life without it). It's important to know what the different possible outcomes are, so that you can work towards specific goals and have informed conversations. After all, you're a business owner now, you need to understand the possible life cycles of a business. But, in the immediate term, your focus should be on establishing, launching, growing your company and making it as profitable as possible. If you're so fixated on the end game that you can't focus on the present, then you are doing your business, your customers, your partner(s) and employees, and ultimately yourself, a disservice.

This chapter is full of some of the most complicated stuff you have to wrap your head around if you want to be an entrepreneur, and it's just a high-level overview. For each topic we've covered there are endless possible deep dives, so if there's a topic you're particularly interested in, you can take a course or read a book on the nitty-gritty, or reach out to someone with expertise in that area. And much of it you will learn on the job, just by getting your hands dirty and doing the work. If you own a business, this will all come up eventually, and one day you'll wake up and realise you know more about running a business than you ever thought possible.

I like to think of all this as a quick and dirty 'what you need to know' for the beginnings of your business, but if you find there's something you don't know and wish you did, follow my lead ... google it! I can't tell you how much time I spent looking up business concepts and reading articles in my earliest entrepreneur days. Every bit of learning helps, and we all have to start somewhere.

7

Mistakes, failures and the 5-second funeral

I never lose. I either win or learn.

NELSON MANDELA

Owning a business will always come with peaks and troughs – you can be up one day and down the next. But as far as I'm concerned, even the 'downs' are opportunities – you will probably learn more when things go 'wrong' than when they go right. Every mistake or unexpected outcome will offer you a tool for your next endeavour, and ultimately you will be more knowledgeable, confident and powerful as a result.

In 2013 – still the early days of A Bikini A Day – Devin and I decided it would be good to have a product to offer to our loyal followers. This was before we'd talked to any manufacturers or knew anything about creating swimsuits, and designing a clothing line seemed like a total pipe dream. Instead, we chose to sell something that seemed logical but also doable: swimsuit calendars. We were two women who posted daily photos in bikinis – that's what our followers came to us for – so a swimsuit calendar was an obvious extension of that content, and it was something tangible that we could sell. We had a captive audience and we wanted to capitalise on that. Plus, this was the time when the Pirelli Calendar and the *Sports Illustrated* Swimsuit Issue were super popular, so it just made sense.

Neither of us knew very much about manufacturing back then. We had no experience in ordering inventory or understanding how much to carry at any given time. We ordered five thousand calendars because ... it seemed like a good number. (We could have benefited from reading this book and learning about those conversion rates!) Our Instagram following had grown from fifteen thousand to nearly three hundred thousand, it was the holidays and we didn't want to run out. In the end, we sold less than half of the calendars, leaving us with about three thousand extras of something that was extremely time-specific. Calendars are not exactly the kind of thing you can resell when the next holiday season comes around.

It wasn't a total disaster. We would go on to make more calendars for A Bikini A Day, but in the later years we made a better job of ordering accurate inventory. That's the point of mistakes, after all. You learn from them and you move on. And there would, of course, be many more endeavours that didn't go as planned: launches that went sideways or employees who didn't work out or products that weren't a hit. But even now, it's hard for me to think of any of these moments as *mistakes*, exactly, because we took away valuable lessons that we incorporated into our future behaviour. As long as you are learning and moving forwards and not repeating the same mistakes over and over, every decision – even the ones that don't work out – has value.

I can't stress enough how important it is to know, going into any entrepreneurial endeavour, that things will go wrong. Of course they will! Ask any successful business owner to tell you the story of how they got to where they are, and I guarantee they will point to a plethora of mistakes and failures that happened along the way. It's an inevitable part of being in business, and if you understand and accept this ahead of time, you will save yourself a lot of heartache and worry. These mess-ups *will* happen: it's normal and it does *not* mean you aren't meant for business or that your company is a bust or that you did anything wrong. Not seeing the opportunities in your failure, or not learning from it ... that's the only true mistake.

The 5-second funeral

Here's a strange confession: I love it when things go wrong. I know, it sounds crazy. But there is so much satisfaction in being a problem-solver. A fixer. There's a rush that comes with that moment when you realise people are looking to you, and even counting on you, to come in and offer leadership and set the tone for how everyone else will respond. I take it almost as a challenge: *Here's the thing that didn't go according to plan, can you make it right?* It feels as if I've been standing around, waiting at the starting line of an upcoming race, and the moment someone says 'there's a problem', I take off running. When it comes down to it, I've realised that I respond so well when things go wrong because it's an opportunity to do right.

At my companies, when something happens that causes my employees to panic – whether someone placed the wrong order with a vendor, or a product didn't turn out the way we intended, or a beloved employee announces she's leaving – I institute what I call the 5-second funeral. It's exactly what it sounds like. Everyone gets five seconds to mope and mourn and freak out, and then we move on. Five seconds of frustration and then it's on to problem-solving. Because, at least in business, every problem can be solved. A bad batch of swimsuits is not a medical emergency. If our server at The Pilates Class is down and our site can't load, it's not a matter of life and death. Keeping that perspective is critical. Your team will follow your lead, so if you're losing your cool, so will they. But if you don't dwell on the mistake, and instead focus on finding a solution as soon as possible, your employees will do the same and they'll take note for the future.

I'm not suggesting that nothing matters, or that you shouldn't care about your company or react when things go wrong. This is your passion project and some mistakes can really hurt. But I promise you, it's better to make these mistakes early, rather than later in the brand's life when the stakes are much higher. Of course you will have feelings, but if you can't handle bumps in the road then you probably aren't cut out for this line of work. Because, like I said, everyone on your team will be watching you to gauge your reaction. In fact, the bigger the crisis, the calmer you need to be. Gather your team and conduct your 5-second funeral. Be honest and transparent about whatever the issue is – if you lie, it *will* get out, and the rumblings of 'What is she trying to hide?' will make everything ten times worse. Then, offer a way forwards. If you don't know what that is just yet, fine, you can and should say as much. 'We have an issue and as a team we will work on a solution to fix it.' It really can be as simple as that.

Step by step

Much more debilitating than any business failure is living in constant fear of failure. Fear is the emotion that will stifle you or incapacitate you. Mistakes reflect action; fear stagnates. It makes the chances of success even smaller. But when you are starting a business and everything is new to you, it's easy to feel overwhelmed. When you feel out of your depth, fear is a natural response.

In the moments when this happens to you, there's really only one solution: make a plan. Take it step by step, and, in each instance, focus on the next step in front of you. You know that saying that a journey of a thousand miles begins with a single step? It's a cliché for a reason. If you do only what's in front of you, and then what's in front of you again, and again, and again ... suddenly you'll look up and realise you have come pretty far.

For me, the fear and overwhelm of running a business feels less like a trek and more like a downhill ski. When I'm at the top of the mountain, it's not just that the journey looks long – it's that it looks terrifying. I want to quit before I start because how on earth can I expect to get down that steep hill without getting hurt? And so, instead of taking in the mountain as a whole and wimping out, I take it moment by moment, staring in front of me but not daring to look at the bottom until it's close in sight.

This is how I approach all the scariest moments in business – whether I'm talking in front of a huge crowd, entering a high-stakes pitch meeting or simply doing something I haven't done before. I focus only on what's directly in front of me. It's simple but it's effective, and it applies to the big stuff *and* the small stuff. If, for you, the metaphorical mountain is simply the idea of starting a business at all, your step by step might start with the list of questions we discussed in the first half of the previous chapter. If, say, you're meeting with potential partners and you're terrified that you'll be too nervous in your meeting, start with step one and break it down as much as you need to:

Step 1: Send the initial kick-off email.

Step 2: Book the space if it's an in-person meeting, or create a Zoom link.

Step 3: Put together a deck with all the relevant information.

Step 4: Practise your presentation.

Step 5: Make a list of any specific requests or action steps you want attendees to leave the meeting with.

Step 6: Order lunch or refreshments for the meeting, if that's necessary.

Step 7: Choose your outfit.

Step 8: Do the meeting.

Step 9: Send a follow-up email, with a thank you note and a summary of any next steps.

By the time you've got to Step 10, you're done! You've stood there, in front of people who may intimidate you, and you've accomplished what you came to do. What's next?

This same approach can be applied to anything. How to find a manufacturer. How to hire a team. How to build a website. How to create a campaign launch. If you think too big-picture, anything new will seem overwhelming, and the fear of making mistakes will stop you in your tracks. But you'll surprise yourself with how far you can go and how much you can achieve if you take it step by step. Just remember to always look back up that mountain and appreciate how far you've come.

The devil is in the details

When it comes to starting a business, very few things are done 'all right' or 'all wrong'. Rarely does anything go perfectly and without a hitch. But it's also pretty unusual for something to be a complete and total disaster. It happens from time to time, sure, but nearly every plan you try to execute will land in that grey area between perfect and failure. It's a big window, which means you have a lot of leeway for mistakes. The skill you, as an entrepreneur, will need to sharpen is the ability to figure out which mistakes matter, and which don't.

Here's something I can tell you right now: as a business owner, you will be busy. Your attention will be pulled in a million different directions. And you'll love that. It's nice to feel needed and to be reminded that you are uniquely qualified to solve the problems that come up. Like I said, it's a rush. But it also requires a fine-tuned ability to manage your time and not let yourself get sidetracked by problems that don't actually matter. A classic rookie mistake when it comes to running a business is getting caught up in insignificant details. And I say this as someone who is quite detail oriented. I'm known for my attention to detail and I think it has helped me get where I am today. But there are details that matter – often the stuff that is customer-facing – and details that don't. For example, when we were launching a pop-up TPC studio in LA, I was the one poring over the details of the space to make sure it felt inviting and serene for customers. But I was also paying attention to parking availability and the restrooms – they may not have been Pilates-related, exactly, but these minor details could have significantly impacted a customer's experience. Using a restroom that feels dirty or gross, or circling for twenty minutes trying to find a parking space, can make an otherwise great Pilates class seem like a pain in the ass. No one is going to return if the parking is a nightmare, especially in a town like Los Angeles where everyone drives everywhere. Yet there are some details that are less important, because they won't affect a user's experience. Being able to identify what's worth your time and energy is a skill in itself. And if you are busy poring over some small detail that ultimately doesn't matter, it means you aren't focusing on something else – potentially the thing that actually *does* matter.

The good news is that the younger your business, the more insignificant the details. Everything can be changed or fixed or solved. When you're just starting out, what matters more than anything is momentum. You want to keep that forward motion going so that you can expand and grow and capitalise on the early excitement. I have seen so many people let amazing ideas linger or businesses die because they dwell on small decisions like a detail on their packaging that someone will probably throw away in five seconds anyway. Or they procrastinate instead of making any decisions at all – like spending months mulling over what their website should look like for launch. The minute you start perseverating, everything slows down. So be decisive, don't get hung up on the small stuff and keep that momentum going!

When your big idea doesn't hit

Have you ever gone on a first date with someone who seemed to be brimming with long-term potential? They are polite, funny, kind, smart ... all the makings of a successful relationship are there. It's not until date five or six that you learn that the jokes you thought were funny get old quite quickly, and the manners you thought were impressive are actually masking a personality that's fairly boring. There was potential, but now you realise this isn't the match for you. But on the bright side, now you have an even better idea of what to look for in The One.

Launching your very first business can sometimes be like those early days of dating. If you have an idea you believe in and are passionate about, of course you're going to think you've hit the jackpot. And you should! If you don't believe in your idea, you aren't giving it the best chance to succeed. But it will very often be the case that your first idea doesn't end up being your *big* idea, and even the most successful people in the world have had times where they lost everything and had to climb their way back to the top. Bill Gates had a failed company that most people have never even heard of before he co-founded Microsoft. Henry Ford had two failed car companies before the Ford Motor Company changed the industry for ever. Jeff Bezos (who has proudly declared he's 'made billions of dollars of failures' at Amazon) had multiple failed ventures before starting Amazon. But even if you're looking for success on a much smaller level – most of us can't expect to be Jeff Bezos or Bill Gates – the first idea likely won't be THE idea. A Bikini A Day, for example, was successful for me and Devin in terms of growth and influence and followers, but it's not where we ended up finding commercial success. Eventually we had to retire that business, because it didn't make sense to keep promoting other brands when we were trying to grow our own. Yes, there's room for everyone, but what we were charging at A Bikini A Day started to feel like small change compared to what we were making with Monday. We had to focus our attention on the side of the business that was the most lucrative, and satisfying, and had the most potential.

If your first big idea doesn't end up being a hit, keep in

mind that the failure of one venture will often push you in the direction of the bigger thing, the one that *is* going to make it. You have to be open to the idea that you'll have to pivot. Who would have thought an online bookstore would become the world's largest online retailer, digital streamer, AI leader and online advertising platform? No one except Jeff Bezos, and I bet even he didn't know it in the beginning. Still, he followed the momentum, was creative and was inventive. All of that is essential.

There's an Albert Einstein quote I absolutely love: 'The measure of intelligence is the ability to change.' Yes! Willingness to see the truth and change as necessary is what will lead to success. You can't be bullish about your idea if you've given it ample time to resonate and grow and the audience just isn't there. Instead of insisting that 'people just don't get it' or 'we just need to stick with it' (assuming enough time has passed), you should be asking, 'OK why didn't this work? What did we learn about what people want, and what they don't want, and how can we adjust accordingly for the next thing?' This is true on a smaller scale as well. If a product isn't working, you need to be willing to accept that and move on or pivot. You can't become too attached to any one idea, and you have to be willing to kill your darlings. Be open to change, get creative and explore all avenues. *That*, more than any success, is the mark of a true entrepreneur.

Redefining failure

If it so happens that your first business is wildly successful, kudos to you! You're a boss and you've accomplished every entrepreneur's dream – amazing! But if you end up (like I did) starting your second or third business, I never want you to feel like you've failed, so let's refine what that means. What makes a business a 'failure'? Is it just that it ceases to exist? If that were the case, you could call A Bikini A Day a failure. It's no longer in operation, after all. But it made money, and it led to bigger opportunities for its founders, and it was our decision to retire it. As I see it, that company is a big-time success story.

The technical definition of a business failure is when a company shuts down due to an inability to turn a profit, or to bring in enough revenue to cover its expenses. But what if those businesses enabled you to start the next one – the successful one – because you took all your learnings and adjusted accordingly? I have worked on a number of companies that no longer exist, none of which I consider a failure. There was Body by Gilles, the fitness company I started with my ex-boyfriend that I stepped away from when we broke up. After I left, the company ceased to operate, but my work there gave me the knowledge I needed to launch another very successful fitness company. There was Andjela, the clothing company that focused on feminine, romantic pieces – the kind of stuff I wear if I'm getting dressed up – which found a loyal audience, but we strategically pivoted away from it in the Covid world where no one left the house and pyjamas become the daytime uniform. Things will happen that are out of your control – a global pandemic was not exactly something we could have planned for – and they will affect your bottom line and your ability to keep a business running.

If you are embarking on a business journey, you might want to take a beat, before you even begin, to consider what you believe qualifies as a failure. Will you be devastated and couch-bound if this particular business isn't your million-dollar idea? No! Try to give yourself permission to redefine 'failure' so that *if* this one isn't your success story, you can take the learnings and move forward without regret and, more importantly, without beating yourself up. Just because something ran its course doesn't mean your experience was without value.

PART 3

Marketing in the new world

8

What consumers care about

What helps people, helps business.

LEO BURNETT

Being a business owner has been one learning opportunity after another. There is so much I didn't know about entrepreneurism and running a company when I first started, and I still surprise even myself when I'm suddenly deep in conversation about EBITDA (see page 264 of the Glossary), profit margins or supply chain logistics. But there is one area of running a business that I've always inherently understood, and that's marketing. I've always known how to generate interest in a product – whether we're talking about my childhood handmade Christmas cards or an Instagram account or an online Pilates class – and I've understood the power of words and images and storytelling to build excitement or curiosity around a brand or service. Looking back on my career, marketing has almost always been at the forefront: my video production company focused on capturing the energy of bars or restaurants so that more people would want to visit. A Bikini A Day was basically a marketing vehicle for other swimsuit brands. By the time I had my own companies that were creating their own products, getting people excited for these products felt like the easy part.

The category of 'marketing' is pretty all-encompassing, and includes a wide range of vehicles you can use to bring attention to your company. We'll get into the different types of marketing – digital, traditional, word of mouth and so on – in the next chapter, but for now, what's important to understand is that marketing is about so much more than just advertising or publicity. It involves positioning your offering so that customers know what you're about, and instilling brand loyalty so that they're proud to use your product or service and will come back again or share with friends.

Marketing is also about establishing who you are as a company, and who your customers are. How you speak to your customer is a major part of that, and I believe that each business should speak to its consumers like the founders would speak to a friend. In social posts and emails, but also in the fine print of packaging, or on the website. There's no detail too small when it comes to establishing your voice. At Monday, for example, we changed the name of our sizing from the very beginning. Instead of the traditional small, medium, large, extra large, we created an entirely new range of sizing we call the V-Range. No one really likes the idea of being called an 'extra large' do they? So instead of L, XL or XXL, we use voluptuous. You might be V, VV or VVV: voluptuous, very voluptuous or very very voluptuous. This is essentially a marketing tactic – it shows the customer who we are, what we are about and that we care about them. It indicates that we had a conversation internally about our customers, and thought intentionally about what they might like or prefer when ordering swimsuits. When it comes to marketing, that is the critical question: what do your customers *want*?

A new approach

The evolution of marketing has always been something I've paid attention to, and it's made a major shift even in my lifetime. Consider the classic Absolut ads, which depicted the now-iconic vodka bottle in various scenes, always with the tagline 'Absolut [something]' (a backyard pool in the shape of an Absolut bottle, for example, with the tagline 'Absolut LA'). Everyone recognised and loved these ads, so by the transitive property, everyone loved Absolut ... even before they could drink it. The campaign was one of the most successful in marketing history – it ran for twenty-five years. The ads worked for a number of reasons, one of which was that they *made* the bottle iconic. They were also all about the product – associating Absolut with cities and landmarks and sports teams and basically whatever was popular in that moment. Plus, they inspired an actual fandom – people would collect the ads and hang them on their walls. That was a success metric in itself, because it's what marketing was all about back then: *everyone's obsessed with this thing, so you should be too.*

The world has changed a lot in the time since those ads (Absolut retired the campaign in 2006), and marketing has had to change with it. People aren't fixated any more on what everyone else is fangirling over (or, at least, they say they aren't). Customers are now focused on how a product or service will *improve their life*. Will it make them feel better? Will it save them time? Will it elevate their game – and that 'game' can be a sport, or cooking, or gardening, or whatever it is they love to do. To really appeal to a wide audience and inspire loyalty, you need to tell your potential customers what *you* can do for *them*.

Put another way: today's marketing, for the most part, is about your customer, not about your brand.

If you have a business idea you're excessively obsessed with, you can probably recite right now five ways your product will improve people's lives. If you didn't think that whatever you're creating is better than the competition, or different in an important way, you probably wouldn't be so excited about it. Maybe your product is multipurpose, so it can do the work of a bunch of products. Great. Now you've saved your consumer time and space and money. Maybe it's a green product, which means your customer is helping the planet and avoiding harsh chemicals. (A word of warning: if you can't think of how your product will improve someone's life – that's important information. Either it's a product the world doesn't need any more of, or at the very least, you're not ready to promote it.) Take The Pilates Class. How do we improve our customers' lives? We provide high-quality, results-based Pilates classes, with some of the world's best trainers, online so that you can take the classes wherever you want. We offer varying lengths of classes, so people can fit fitness into their busy schedules, but the classes themselves feel luxurious and calming. And there's enough variety that anyone can find a class that works for them – our tagline is 'For Every Body'.

It's important to be honest with yourself and be really clear about why your product or service will make your customers' lives easier. Consumers are smart. They can tell when your brand story is authentic, and more importantly they can sniff out a fake marketing ploy. Authenticity means that you aren't making up a story that you think your customers want to hear, or putting out messages that don't actually reflect who you are or what your business is about. An authentic brand lives its values. Whatever it markets as important, it is incorporating behind the scenes too. If you say as a brand that diversity is important, for example, you are hiring a diverse workforce and respecting diverse voices internally and keeping diversity in mind when you create products. You're not just blowing smoke or saying something to make yourself look good. If you don't believe whatever story you're telling about your product, neither will your customers. This is where Monday really excelled. No one believed in our swimwear more than Devin and I did. We had worn thousands of bikinis from brands all over the world by the time we started selling swimsuits. We knew what was out there, and that a lot of it didn't work. We knew that when you wear a swimsuit that fits poorly or digs into your skin, it can make you feel anxious or self-conscious or uncomfortable ... the exact opposite of what you should be feeling at the beach. Going to the beach should be about relaxing and spending time with people you love. There should be no insecurity or worry surrounding what's supposed to be a beautiful and stress-free experience, and that's the message we wanted to impart to our customers – that when you put on our swimwear, it fits so well, and the fabric is so high quality, that nothing is pulling or poking you where it shouldn't be. You will be happier in your body, and thus happier at the beach. And there's a lot of value there, especially in a space like swimwear, which can be so fraught for women.

Our earliest marketing showcased our message of celebrating women – every photo and post and piece of brand content highlighted our love for ourselves and our bodies, for each other, and really for all women and all women's bodies. We were promoting body acceptance long before it was trendy to do so, because we have always genuinely believed that all women's bodies are beautiful – if you're good on the inside, you are perfect on the outside. The story of Monday was a story of confidence, and it was important to us that our audience understood that if you wear our products, you will feel beautiful and confident. In a swimsuit! That's a pretty major life improvement for most women.

But that's one company's story. It's how we at Monday intended to make our customers' lives better. Depending on what your business is, your story will be very different. Let's say you're selling a garden hose. You probably aren't going to have a big, inspiring message around your product – it's not going to suddenly make someone feel beautiful, and if you tried to say as much, consumers would mock you. Remember, people can sniff out BS. In the garden hose situation, you have to focus on what practical advantages you bring to the table. Are you more efficient than the traditional hose? Well, that's pretty major, both for the person looking to save time and the person looking to save water. Are you more flexible, and thus easier to use? That matters too. Do you take up a lot less space in a cramped garage than what people have been using for ages? Perfect. The point is, every company's marketing message will be different, but they all should answer the same core question for your customers: 'What will you do for me?'

Of course, there are still brands – especially luxury brands – that lean into their roles as status symbols and don't necessarily embrace 'life improvement' marketing. I would be lying if I pretended that there weren't any businesses that exist purely for consumerism. But customers are becoming more savvy, and they are less interested in wasteful and unnecessary products or brands. So if you're considering starting a business that's focused on a product that's wasteful or unnecessary, just for your own profit, I encourage you to think again. That's just not the direction in which the world is moving, and it's far less fulfilling too. I get the most satisfaction out of owning something that I genuinely believe makes a difference, and I guarantee you will too.

The golden age of marketing

There has never been a better time to be an entrepreneur. Digital tools like Zoom and Shopify have simplified the once-complicated tasks of connecting with remote employees or building an online sales platform. Start-up costs are shrinking – people are trading office space for remote set-ups – while readily available virtual help in areas like payroll and HR makes it easy to outsource those responsibilities until you can afford to hire in-house. But one of the very best bonuses of going into business today is that you control your own marketing. You can get your brand story out there even if you're a so-called 'little guy'.

Before social media became a hub for brand marketing, and before tech made it easy to own your own marketing campaigns, businesses generally had to pay outside firms to come up with their marketing ideas. The takeaway often boiled down to 'whichever company has the most money wins'. Success meant getting your product into a magazine, and that was largely a game of 'Who do you know?' Marketing firms certainly still exist, and if you're willing or able to spend you can benefit from their expertise. But there's so much more opportunity these days to market without spending a fortune. The tools to create your own marketing campaigns are out there, and they are more affordable than ever. You can use your own social media platforms (no matter how small they are – you've got to start somewhere!), you can create virtual focus groups, you can partner with other small businesses, you can connect with influencers, you can send marketing emails, you can even send follow-up emails to those who clicked-through the first email but never purchased. You can do giveaways that require followers to tag friends, thereby increasing your audience. The days of crossing your fingers and hoping you make it into the September issue of *Vogue* or 'Oprah's Favorite Things' are gone. (Don't get me wrong, if you can make those things happen, all the better, but it won't break you if you can't.)

All of this is great news for the small business that is prepared to make its mark. The opportunities to make a major impact with even a small investment are there. But, as is usually the case, with great opportunity comes great responsibility. Customers are more involved than ever in their purchasing decisions. They want to know who and where they are buying from, and they hold the businesses they patronise to extremely high standards. This is ultimately a good thing – it rewards companies with sound and ethical business practices. But it means you need to stand behind your decisions, and not launch your marketing campaigns until you are confident in your practices. The consumer has more power than ever – cancel culture is real – and they *will* hold you accountable, so you'd better not only believe in your product but also know how it's made and feel confident in how you are marketing it. Forgoing the outside firm means passing on an external temperature check. Accountability is good, but you have to be ready for it.

What I'm trying to say is, there is more marketing opportunity now than ever ... but don't take that for granted. You'll hear me say this one a lot: do it right, or don't do it at all.

KISS

Perhaps you've heard of the acronym KISS. Originally a design principle, it stands for 'Keep It Simple, Stupid' – basically, it cautions against overcomplicating something. This concept can be applied to so many areas of business (and life!), but I often come back to it in regards to marketing. In branding, online content, websites, emails ... simplicity is key across the board. Convey your message to your customer as if you are talking to a five-year-old, not because your customer is dumb (I assure you, customers are savvier than ever) but because everyone is busy.

There is an incredible amount of content vying for an individual's attention at any one time, and the average human attention span is getting increasingly shorter. In fact, research conducted by Dr Gloria Mark, a professor at the University of California, Irvine, and author of *Attention Span: A Groundbreaking Way to Restore Balance, Happiness and Productivity*, found that the average adult could pay attention to a screen for two and a half minutes (or 150 seconds) in 2004. By 2023, the average attention span when looking at a screen had shrunk to forty-seven seconds, but in truth, unless your content is engaging you'll struggle to get someone past fifteen seconds. If your marketing story is long and complicated – even if it's really clever or funny – you will lose people. You still want to stand out and be creative, but not at the expense of being clear. Your customer should be able to understand your marketing story at first glance, because they are not going to expend energy trying to decipher it. The same is true for any actions you want them to take: make purchasing your product or ordering your service as easy as humanly possible. If your customer needs to spend time figuring out where to click to subscribe or how to add something to their cart, I promise you they will give up and move on to a website that's easier to use. Do not sacrifice ease and simplicity, no matter how cool and innovative you think your new approach is. Online behaviour is learned and instinctive, and consumers are not trying to change their habits.

If you're marketing your product largely or even entirely online – which is increasingly the case (business forecasters predict that e-commerce will soon account for 25 per cent of global retail sales) – you have to remember that you're asking someone to make what might feel, to them, like a blind purchase. Sure, they can look at photographs or watch videos on your website and read reviews online, but they usually can't hold the product in their hand or see it in person or, if we're talking about clothes or accessories, try it on before buying. Those kinds of sensory experiences are important because they evoke emotion – trying on a dress that fits just right can spark joy; smelling a fragrance can transport you back to the comfort of childhood; feeling a soft blanket can make you feel immediately relaxed and cosy. Your job, when marketing online, is to do everything you can – while still keeping it simple – to evoke a similarly sensory experience in your customer.

At Monday, we've found that the suits made from our textured fabrics sell better because they look more three-dimensional and substantive in photos. If you're marketing a vacuum cleaner, on the other hand, you'll want to give your customers the satisfaction of seeing the product suck up dirt and grime. Jewellery needs to be sparkling and shining in all your marketing content. It doesn't matter what you're selling, when your customers have a visceral reaction to your product, their desire to purchase it will be rooted in emotion rather than too much thought. Clarity plus an emotional experience will usually equal a customer.

Know your audience

I mentioned in Chapter 6 the importance of understanding the demographics of your audience. As you begin to gather information about your consumer, perhaps through surveys or focus groups, here's some specific information you might want to collect that can help inform business decisions and product development (you may not need to know all of this, but as you build your business you'll get a sense of which information feels relevant):

- gender
- age
- birthdate
- ethnicity
- location
- marital status
- household income
- education
- employment status
- language
- family and dependants
- clothing size.

The more information you can gather about your typical customer, the better you can tailor your marketing messaging to meet their needs. But to really speak to your audience, you might have to go deeper, doing what you can to really understand their needs and moods. I am based between Australia and the US, but my business is entirely based in Los Angeles and the majority of our customers are in the States. That means I need to know what's going on politically in the

US at all times, because those issues affect my customers. Paying attention to the world around you – even when you're immersed in launching a business, which can feel like your own little bubble of isolation – is so important. It can protect you from launching a campaign that's tone-deaf, for example, which can get you cancelled before you even start.

The more you can get into the minds of your customers, the better. If you cater to a Gen Z audience, for example, you want to have a finger on the pulse of whatever issues are important to them. You want to know what they are watching and reading and listening to, what video games they are playing, which celebrities or activists they admire. What concerns do they have? What do they value, and what do they *not* value? This kind of information can inform so much about the story you will tell about your product. If you have a fitness company that incorporates community as part of its platform, for example, your marketing could be all about how it will make your customer stronger and more badass, or it could focus on the connection piece – that it will bring users together with others who have similar goals. Both could be effective marketing campaigns. It all depends on what your audience wants.

Gathering all this information takes work. There's the classic market research, like the surveys and focus groups I've already mentioned (more on page 210), but you will also need to know the publications, influencers and blogs and TikToks and YouTube channels that your audience follows. You can ask for this information in your surveys, or you can use audience analyser or customer analytics tools that can gather this information for you. You'll need to pay attention to news stories and trend pieces. Attitudes towards work, for example, have changed so much over the past few years – they differ between generations, and they differ now from how they were before the pandemic. If you are marketing a career-related service, understanding those differences is key. Maybe the marketing changes from a 'hustle culture'-focused approach to one that recognises that 'work isn't life, but you might as well be happy/comfortable/productive while you're there'. The options for storytelling are endless, but knowing what's going on, at a high level, in the lives of your audience is non-negotiable.

But here's the kicker: your audience is made up of people. Behind the demographic data and think pieces about Gen Z or millennials or Gen X, are actual human beings, and human beings change. They grow. And so do their needs or interests. One marketing campaign won't work for ever, because the needs – and wants – of your customer will evolve. When Devin and I launched Monday, we captured an audience that was very similar to us in terms of age but also in terms of priorities and interests. Like us, our audience enjoyed small luxuries and cared about health and wellness and wanted to be in beautiful surroundings. There was a lot of glamour and wanderlust and friendship showcased in our marketing, because it's what we were about and what our audience was about. That was ten years ago. A lot can happen in a decade, and the original Monday customer has grown up right alongside us. That doesn't mean we change our tune entirely – we still speak to the twenty-five to thirty-five-year-olds who make up our core customer base, and we make sure to invest in the social platforms where they are, even if that's not where we started. We know we perform in that demo and we always want to maintain that base even if we are ageing out of that window ourselves. But we're also broadening the range of what we do, in part because our customer base is broadening too. When we started Monday, it would never have occurred to us to make maternity wear because we didn't wear it and neither did our customers. But now, ten years later, many of our loyal customers need maternity suits, and they don't want to sacrifice quality or feeling beautiful in their body just because they are pregnant. Why would they? Our audience has grown, and as a result so has Monday.

Staying top of mind

Top-of-mind, or front-of-mind, awareness, is the notion that you want your company and product to be the first one that comes up for a consumer when they think about your industry. So, when people are asked about soda, for example, Coca-Cola wants those people to immediately think of Coca-Cola rather than Pepsi. When women think of swimsuits, we want them to think of Monday first.

Front-of-mind awareness is why you don't stop marketing even if your company is on top. Let's go back to that soda example. Coca-Cola has been the most popular soda worldwide for decades. If the goal was just to get on top, it could have stopped marketing ages ago. Instead, the soda giant spends billions of dollars on marketing each year. Billions! That's because it wants to stay top of mind, and if another company is marketing like crazy while Coca-Cola is taking a break, it could lose that positioning.

When you are just starting your business, you will not be the first company that comes to a customer's mind no matter what space you're in. You're just too new. But understanding that goal, and its importance to marketing, can help drive your campaigns. It will remind you that the overall goal of marketing isn't to cater to a specific event or focus on a specific season or sell a specific product. Those might be smaller, individual goals, but the overarching goal should be to drive brand awareness and brand loyalty, so customers will keep coming back.

In order to increase your brand awareness and become more top of mind for your customers, keep in mind the 'rule of seven', a marketing principle that's been around since the 1930s and is often credited to Hollywood movie executives: customers need to see your brand at least seven times before they will commit to making a purchase. (When it was originally conceived, the 'rule' was about how often moviegoers would need to see a film poster before buying a ticket.) Even if you've done everything right and shared a compelling story about how your product will change and improve your customer's life in a way that will resonate with them, they are unlikely to click that 'buy now' button the first time they learn about your product. Or the second time. Or third. Again, it takes about *seven* times to really convince them, which means you need to be marketing in various channels and probably doing more than you think you should. You probably operate in the same way as a consumer of the brands you love, even if you don't realise it. But the point is, this is not an area where you need to worry about overkill. More really is more.

Staying top of mind – and the rule of seven – is also why it's so important to commit to marketing year-round, even if yours is a company with a very seasonal product or service. At Monday we don't only market in the summer, and if I ran a snowsuit company I wouldn't only market in the winter. I want people to see us all year, so when the time comes to buy a suit, they aren't racking their brain thinking, *What's the name of that company? The one with the cute suits I saw on social?* I don't want to have to reintroduce customers to what we do or remind them of who we are, which is why at Monday, marketing in winter is just as important as it is in spring or summer.

Spin cycle

Ultimately, marketing is spin. It's about positioning your product in whatever way will best serve your customer and convince them that they want what you are selling. Now, to be clear, that doesn't mean you lie, or say that your product can do something it can't. Your marketing message should be genuine, because as we know, customers know when something is inauthentic. But as we've discussed, the more you can hype up what you believe to be true about your brand, the more likely it is that your customers will ultimately believe it too.

If you have an audience that wants luxury, for example, it's not just about what you say in your marketing message but *how* you market. Consumers will equate certain milestones with success. A feature in *Vogue*, for example, or a billboard in Times Square. When people see those things, in person or even just a picture online, they will infer that your offering is premium or that your brand is successful due to its popularity. Consider the billboard. We put a Monday billboard up in New York City, but I didn't really care as much if people on the streets of New York saw it. I cared more about the people who saw on social media that Monday was on an NYC billboard – we posted beautiful pics of the billboard and celebrated it and shared it and created a social moment around it – because those people were likely to develop a higher regard for the brand as a result. Once they see that, *Oh this brand was on a billboard*, maybe they believe that these swimsuits they've been coveting will not only improve their lives but do so with a bit of luxury. It's hard to track the return on investment for something like a billboard, but that doesn't mean you shouldn't put up the billboard. You just want to maximise the storytelling and get the absolute biggest bang for your buck. If you can amplify the billboard on social media, so people around the world see it rather than just the people in one city, now you've elevated the brand on a global scale. That should be the consistent goal around all your marketing: maximising your marketing spend rather than throwing ads or billboards out into the world and hoping they work. That way you're giving your audience a story they care about while getting yourself the recognition you need.

9

Which marketing approach is right for you?

You can't sell anything if you can't tell anything.

BETH COMSTOCK

As you can probably tell, I believe wholeheartedly in the power of marketing. Especially in this day and age, when so much purchasing is happening online and every company is trying to steal customer attention, brand awareness is so important. After all, if your business is entirely e-commerce, you can't depend on foot traffic or serendipitous discovery. You need to find a way to break through the noise so that your customers know you're out there. You might have an incredible product, but consumers can't buy what they don't know about.

At all of my brands, marketing is one of our top investments. But that money isn't earmarked for any one particular channel; it goes towards a variety of strategies that we think will capture the most attention. In order for any company to get the biggest return on its marketing investment, it needs to diversify. If you put all your eggs in one basket, you aren't maximising your chances of success. Especially when it's early in your business's lifespan, there's no way to know exactly what strategy – or strategies – will be the most effective. By approaching your marketing from various angles, you can gather data on what works (there are endless tools to tell you how a customer found you or where they clicked through from) and what doesn't, and increase your chance of getting in front of as wide an audience as possible. And since we know an audience needs to see something at least seven times before actually purchasing, diversifying your marketing allows you to hit that lucky number seven more quickly. That said, there are more marketing channels and strategies than any single company can employ, or even *should* employ. If you diversify *too* much, you risk diluting your budget and not getting the maximum return from any marketing tactic.

Getting that 'just right' breakdown depends on your product, your audience and your budget, among other factors. So how do you figure out which marketing approach is right for you?

Well, let's take a step back and start at the beginning ...

Marketing 101

As I mentioned in the previous chapter, marketing is about bringing attention to and raising awareness of whatever it is you are selling. It's an umbrella term, and although it is often confused with areas like advertising or PR, each of these actually falls under that marketing umbrella. The list of the various marketing sub-specialities seems to be constantly growing, but it includes:

- content marketing
- advertising

- public relations
- branding
- events
- product marketing
- influencer/celebrity marketing.

Within these areas, you can drill down even further into specific channels – tactics like email marketing or social media marketing or search engine marketing are what we'll be focusing on in this chapter – but as you begin to consider your company's marketing budget, keep in mind that you'll want to allocate money for most, if not all, of these areas. Branding – developing the look of your logo or packaging – is important because design sends a message about your business. Events could include any pop-up shops you launch or, if you are a services company, in-person gatherings you might have for your loyal customers. Public relations (PR) is the department you might call on if there is a crisis and you need to give a statement, or you need to secure press attention and media placements for your brand with their plethora of contacts. PR is usually not paid for (it's often called 'earned media' for that reason), unlike many other areas of marketing that usually are. Depending on your business, you might not need to spend on PR. Or you may not have any events. Most likely, you'll grow into some of these areas as your business grows.

Marketing has changed in countless ways in recent decades. Yes, there is the change in focus from the brand to the consumer, but the *channels* through which companies market have also evolved drastically. When I think about what marketing looks like for my companies, I think less about the subsections listed above and focus more on the specific channels I can use to speak to my customers. Those channels tend to fall into two categories: traditional and digital marketing.

Traditional marketing includes all the seemingly old-school marketing tactics you probably remember from your childhood. Print ads, TV commercials, mailers, ads on bus shelters. Those methods are still around and still work, but they can be expensive, and their effectiveness can be hard to measure. Digital marketing is what it sounds like – marketing through digital channels like social media platforms, search engines, email, websites. Digital marketing is more affordable than traditional marketing, it's easier to track the ROI (return on investment), and considering that online reference library DataReportal's 2022 Global Overview Report found that the average person spent more than six and a half hours a day online in 2022, it meets your customers where they are.

Traditional vs digital marketing channels

The lists below are not exhaustive (and there's plenty more to learn about any of these methods that may interest you), but having a baseline understanding of these different types of marketing will come in handy as you start thinking through how to allocate your marketing funds. Think of this as an entry-level marketing dictionary, so you can have the conversation without googling under the table. (Although, if it does come to that, no shame. Been there.)

Traditional

- Broadcast: TV commercials, radio ads
- Direct mail: catalogues, brochures, postcards, flyers

- Handouts: flyers or brochures distributed in person in public areas
- Outdoor: billboards, bulletin boards, buses and bus shelters, posters
- Print: magazine ads, newspaper ads
- Telemarketing: cold calls
- Window displays: displays in a store window that potential customers can see from the street
- Word of mouth: when customers share or recommend a product in conversation

Digital

- Analytics: tracking user behaviour online in order to gather data and tailor content to specific customers
- Affiliate: when someone (an 'affiliate') promotes a brand and receives a small commission for each sale that comes from their recommendation (affiliates usually have specific affiliate links or codes, so that the sale can be tracked to them)
- Email: emails sent to customers or potential customers promoting your product
- Mobile: text (SMS) messages or mobile notifications to customers reminding them of a sale or to complete a purchase
- Search engine marketing: ads on a search engine like Google, Yahoo! or Bing
- Search engine optimisation (SEO): tailoring your content to include high-frequency search terms so that you rank higher in search results

- Social media: posts on Facebook, Instagram, TikTok, Pinterest, YouTube, etc., which can be seen by your followers
- Paid social: ads on platforms like Facebook, Instagram, TikTok, Pinterest, YouTube, etc., which are served to those who don't necessarily follow your social accounts
- Influencer partnerships (paid and unpaid): posts by social media influencers who are not directly associated with the brand but have a strong following who are more likely to buy a product if an influencer endorses it.

There is no hard-and-fast rule about how much of your revenue you should budget for marketing. The US Small Business Administration suggests that most small businesses should allocate 7–8 per cent of their revenue to marketing. I tend to believe in doubling that if your business allows it. Obviously, before your business launches you will have no revenue, but if there's money in your start-up budget to allocate to marketing, you won't be sorry. The returns from your marketing efforts feed directly back into your revenue, so it's a powerful investment.

Choosing your marketing channels

Given the plethora of marketing channels available, it's reasonable that you might feel overwhelmed by the various options. Keep in mind that this is a good problem to have. New age marketing is extensive, but it means you can market your brand no matter how fledgling your company or how small your budget. It's no longer a luxury reserved for the wealthy or well connected.

At Monday, our marketing efforts started with only Instagram, email and Facebook. We were exclusive to those platforms – on Instagram and Facebook we relied first on our own social posts, and in year two we added paid ads. (Both paid off: we had an incredibly strong launch on the reach of our organic social audience alone, but when we employed paid ads, our sales doubled.) Our emails went out to those who ordered from us, as well as to those who'd signed up to get information about launches and sales. Over time, as our revenue grew – and thus our operating budget grew – so too did our marketing reach. Today we still utilise those original platforms, but we've expanded to include outdoor ads and print advertising, and we're on more social platforms, including TikTok, Pinterest and YouTube.

For a young company, digital marketing is where you'll probably want to start. (Digital marketing, as you can see from the list on the previous page, is about more than social media, but social media is only getting more important. If you want to learn more about it right away, go straight to page 199, where I break down the nuances of social for an entire chapter.) The power of the digital medium is, simply put, incredible. Why?

- It's less expensive.
- You get a big bang for your buck.
- You can reach a wider, and often a more targeted, audience.
- It's measurable.

Let's look at those last two benefits in a little more detail . . .

Wider, more targeted audience

With paid social ads, for example, you can tailor which audience gets served your promotion, which is not the case with a magazine or TV ad. Sure, you can pick a show or a magazine with a similar audience to yours, but you can't drill down with the same amount of detail as you can with an Instagram ad, where you can choose an age range or location. And people spend so much time scrolling, you have more hours to get in front of your potential customers.

Measurable

By measurable, I mean that you can collect detailed data on which posts or emails convert to clicks and, even better, to sales. You can A/B test ads (which means you run the same advertisement with one or more variables, to see which gets more clicks), or you can track specific links in emails to figure out which are getting clicked on and which are ignored. Not to mention, if you're selling your product online, digital marketing includes direct links. You don't have to tell people a URL and hope they remember it, or repeat your brand name over and over – it's easier than ever to convert a user into a customer.

How to pick 'em

During your start-up days, don't worry about being on every platform. Pick two or three channels to start and be very smart about it. The channels you choose should depend on a number of factors:

- **What are you selling? To whom?** At Monday, The
  Pilates Class or The Birthing Class, we don't have
  a big LinkedIn marketing presence because that's
  not where our audience is. When you're perusing
  LinkedIn, you're thinking about your career, you're
  not there looking for beachwear or fitness classes. Yes,
  of course professionals wear bathing suits and work
  out too, but the in-the-moment focus of a LinkedIn
  user is on career: either finding a job or networking or
  professional development. As a business, you want to
  capture the attention of your audience when they're
  in the mindset to positively receive your message. If I
  owned a company that offered online classes, on the
  other hand – something like, say, MasterClass – then
  LinkedIn advertising might make a lot more sense.
- **The age of your customer.** Companies targeting younger
  users might choose to pass on email in favour of SMS
  (text) marketing. As I write this book, Facebook, for
  example, has an older audience, while TikTok speaks
  to a much younger user. But this is constantly evolving.
  Social media is still such a young space that new
  platforms pop up all the time, while once popular ones
  shut down or rebrand. The platforms that are all the
  rage with younger audiences suddenly become old news
  if something shinier catches on. Your marketing strategy
  can't be a one-and-done decision. Your marketing
  mix should change alongside the digital preferences of
  your customers. (If you are targeting a senior citizen
  population – a rapidly growing demographic – you
  may even find that it makes sense to allocate some of
  your earliest budget to traditional channels like print
  newspaper ads, because the average age of a newspaper
  reader is steadily increasing.)

- **Location of your target audience.** If your business is hyperlocal, radio ads or handing out flyers might be a strategic slice of your marketing pie. If it's global, digital has a broader reach. Every business will have a different logical make-up of its marketing channels, based on factors specific to that business. It's a matter of thinking strategically and remaining nimble enough to make changes as necessary.

The ever-changing digital landscape

Even if you do everything 'right' with your digital marketing approach, you are still, at some level, at the mercy of whatever platform or channel you're marketing on. If Google or Instagram or TikTok or whatever newfangled social media platform is huge in twenty years makes a change internally, your content will be affected, whether it's paid advertisements or organic social content. Perhaps you know someone in marketing and you've heard them complain about how a platform 'updated its algorithm'. This happens across social media sites, and what it means, essentially, is that a platform has changed its formula for deciding who sees what content. The idea is that as the platforms get smarter about what users do and do not like, they can do a better job of giving each user only the content they want to see. This is, at least in theory, a positive for the user, and an improvement in terms of their experience. But for marketers, it can be a giant headache. Consider Instagram, for example. If that platform changes its algorithm, it could mean that a brand that previously knew how to create content that landed in the feeds of its intended audience suddenly needs to shift strategies because the same approach is now getting fed to far fewer people, which could gravely affect sales. Giving you an understanding of any one specific algorithm is certainly not the intent of this chapter – that information is constantly changing – but I do want you to understand that, in some ways, marketing on social involves putting your success in someone else's hands. These platforms have a lot of control. That doesn't mean you shouldn't use them. They are still the best option for a young company looking to capture an audience and build a following. But it's another reason why you need to diversify – if you invest entirely in one channel or strategy, there's a lot of crossing your fingers involved, hoping that an algorithm doesn't change . . . or scrambling if it does.

These types of large-scale changes aren't just about social media. Changes can also come from companies like Apple or Google. You may think your business has nothing to do with these tech giants, but if everyone is accessing your business via their iPhones or Androids, you are inextricably linked to their software. An example: before Apple instituted a policy requiring users to explicitly give permission for apps or websites to track their activity, whenever a user came across the Monday website, we could track their behaviour to understand what they buy, what is in their cart, whether they convert to a customer when they click on an ad, and the general return on investment in terms of marketing dollars. Today, companies are not allowed to track a user without their permission, so we only have about half the data we used to in terms of customer behaviour. These updates are not bad, necessarily, but they're just another reminder that you can't rely on any single method because, especially in the digital marketing world, things can change on a dime. A strategy you rely on one day can look completely different the next. The takeaway? Choose your channels wisely and be loyal to what you know is converting, but always diversify, and always remain agile. The minute you settle in and get comfortable is when something will change.

Go big or go home

Marketing is what you make of it. You can pay big bucks for an ad in *Vogue* in the hope that your audience sees it when it comes out, or you can pay the big bucks and not only get the ad in *Vogue* but also share a photo of the ad in your social feeds and include a shout-out to that achievement in your next email and ask your friends to share it whenever they see it. As a business owner, you want to maximise the efficiency of all your efforts, and that's true for marketing perhaps more than anything. I won't generally advocate for a never-be-satisfied mindset, but that really is how you have to think of this area of the business. For every piece of promotion, ask yourself, 'What else can I get out of this? How can I get it in front of more eyes? How can I celebrate it and make it seem like a big deal, no matter what it is?'

Remember that NYC billboard I mentioned in the previous chapter? Sure, I wanted to catch the eyes of potential customers walking down the street in New York City, but, like I said, the bigger goal was to continue establishing ourselves as the kind of premium brand that has a billboard in New York City. So how did we maximise efficiency? Well, first of all, we waited until the business was about four years old. Launching our company with a billboard wouldn't have made a lot of sense – it would have been expensive and we didn't yet have a big enough audience for them to particularly care that we had a billboard. When the time came that we could afford it, and we had the audience to appreciate it, we really blew it up. We had the billboard, but then we hired a photographer to take photos of the billboard, we made videos of the big billboard reveal and of Devin and I seeing ourselves on the billboard and of people walking past it, and members of our team posted it on their social feeds. We squeezed all the juice out of that campaign that we possibly could.

The billboard is just one of hundreds of techniques we've implemented at Monday, but in general I try to train my team to think in terms of an omnichannel approach to any marketing moment. I'll talk more about social media launches in the next chapter, but in general I like to think of any major marketing moment as a tree with many branches. If I'm launching a new swimsuit collection, I would never just post it on Instagram and call it a day. We want to create as many chances as possible for our audience to see it, so at the bare minimum we post it on the homepage of our website, our Instagram feed, our Stories, send an email and/or SMS, do a Facebook post and gift the product to influencers in the hope that they will post. That really is just the minimum – most campaigns also involve digital advertising of the product, potentially a paid influencer partnership (more on that on page 191), a billboard, a podcast ad, and sometimes we even plan a corresponding event that we also share through all the aforementioned channels. It took me a while to get my teams to see the bigger picture and understand that since so much effort goes into creating certain products or classes, a simple social media post won't cut it. There are so many ways to get creative without spending a lot, so make sure you really are going big or going home when it comes to product promotion.

I know you might be asking yourself, 'Isn't that a little bit annoying? Won't users get sick of my company if we're hyping everything up so much?' But remember that just because you, as the business owner, are seeing each piece of content you create and you may feel like you're overdoing it . . . I promise you're not. Most users won't see every piece of content. Stories come and go on social. Feeds are constantly being updated. Maximising efficiency means maximising your chances of getting in front of people and maximising the odds that they'll remember you. In between seeing, for example, the photo of your billboard and the video of it and the other video and the *other* photo, your user is scrolling through a zillion ads or posts from other companies. It might seem to you like it's all *you're* seeing, but for your user that's simply not the case. Always err on the side of doing more.

Word of mouth

If I had to pick, I would say that the absolute best kind of marketing you can hope for is word of mouth – people who love your product telling their friends about it, who then tell *their* friends, and so on, until you are a runaway success. Of course it never happens quite that quickly and easily, but that's the idea. Word-of-mouth marketing is the most effective in terms of translating to sales, but it's also the toughest to achieve, because you can't buy it. The only way to build the kind of buzz that's needed for word-of-mouth sales is to have a really good product.

At the end of the day, word of mouth will keep you honest. So much about marketing is spin, as you already know, and if you have a really strong marketing strategy, you might be able to sell a product even if it isn't any good. Of course, selling something once won't keep you in business. You need return customers, and if your offering is a piece of crap, no one is going to shell out cash for it more than once. But word of mouth – you can't even get that started without a really strong product, one that your customers are so passionate about they just have to share it with friends. And here's the other thing: word of mouth works two ways. Just as someone is going to tell their bestie when they finally find *the* perfect white T-shirt or lipstick or swaddle blanket for their baby, they are absolutely going to tell their bestie if they bought something that turned out to be absolute crap. We want our friends to know about the amazing products or services we use, and we also want to protect them from the bad ones. So as much as word of mouth can work for you, it can also work against you, and that can be the kiss of death.

What makes word of mouth so valuable? Well, let me ask you this: what do you trust more, a recommendation from a commercial or from your close friend? If a sunglasses company tells you that its frames won't slip, always look great *and* are inexpensive, are you swayed? What about if that same description came from your sister? Consumers may be convinced by good marketing, but it takes time, because a company's official social channels aren't exactly a trusted source.

Even a neutral source is better than one connected to your company. Word-of-mouth recommendations don't have to come from your friends or family members. Customer reviews – on your website or Amazon or Yelp – matter because, first of all, anything with thousands of five-star reviews speaks for itself. You can't get that many people to leave positive reviews unless they are really passionate. Also, even if you don't know the person, a 'regular person' leaving a review carries more weight than someone connected with the brand, which is why you as a business owner want to make it easy for satisfied customers to leave positive reviews. But truly nothing is better than a personal recommendation. Once a friend tells me I absolutely need something, or raves about how much she loves it, it's a sure thing I'm going to try it for myself. So anything you can do to improve your chances of building word-of-mouth buzz – incentivising happy customers to share, reminding return customers to leave reviews – is worth it.

The power of influencers

A recommendation from an influencer you don't know personally may not be as convincing as one from a close friend, but if you've been following a specific influencer for a while you may *feel* like you know them. You might also trust their recommendations, either because you like their style or because you've successfully bought other products they've featured. For small businesses, influencers with loyal followings can have a huge impact, and as a result they might be an incredibly valuable paid marketing channel for you to consider (though payment isn't always necessary).

For the first five years of Monday, we did not engage in any paid influencer partnerships. We simply gifted swimsuits to influencers who genuinely loved the brand. At some point, though, we had so many new collections launching that we needed to work with content creators and influencers in a paid partnership to ensure they would create content for the drops ahead of time. In the summer, for example, we have a new product drop almost every week, sometimes two. If we gifted that product to an influencer, with no payment, and just hoped she featured it, it might take weeks for her to wear the product organically and post about it. By then, we would have moved on to the next drop, which would make the influencer's post far less valuable. Instead, we started to engage a diverse group of influencers to wear and shoot the items, and part of the agreement was that they would post on or during the week of launch.

We test our paid influencer partnerships through multiple different metrics. We may have them share a code that allows us to directly track the return on our investment, but that depends on the influencer and the audience – we always want our partnerships to feel as organic as possible. For an influencer partnership to be successful, we've learned that this person needs to (a) genuinely love the brand, (b) create content that is organic to our audience and doesn't feel 'pushy', and (c) create captions and content that are aligned with our voice. But a partnership goes both ways, and we give influencers the creative licence to do what they think will resonate based on their knowledge of their followers. After all, there is a reason they have a loyal following – they know what their audience wants.

Working with an influencer isn't always about ROI. It might be that a post doesn't get huge engagement on their page or translate to a high number of purchases, but then we share their post on our page and our customers really resonate with it. Some influencers might represent our brand beliefs and highlight things we are proud of, like the eco-friendly elements of the brands, the diversity or a charitable cause. Like any successful partnership, not every influencer collab will be a hit – but when it works, it really works.

The importance of sales promotions

When I first started Monday, I specifically remember saying 'I never want to put our brand on sale.' I believed our range was so premium that it didn't deserve to be sold at a discount. I've since heard a lot of new business owners say something similar, but I was wrong and so are they. Sales promotion is a very important part of nearly every business, and a marketing strategy in itself. First of all, remember all that redundant inventory I spoke about earlier? Sales are your way to clear it out without having to dispose of it in a wasteful way like incinerating it (yes, that's a thing that many businesses do). No matter how amazing your inventory planner, you will always have leftover stock. Second of all, sales give those who love your brand but can't afford to invest in a full-priced item a chance to purchase. This is a whole customer base in itself – maybe they *can* afford your products, but they are just careful with their money and prefer to buy only when something is on sale. And, finally, some of the biggest days of the year in terms of any business's revenue are sales days. Black Friday in the US, Boxing Day in Australia and the UK, and Singles' Day in China. If you don't participate you could see a serious decline in sales that day while your customers spend their money somewhere else. That doesn't mean you should hold a sale every time you need a boost, because sales that are too frequent can have the opposite effect. If your customers get used to very frequent sales promotions, gifts with purchase or discount codes, they may decide to hold off buying your full-priced items entirely. Bottom line, unless you are Louis Vuitton you will need to implement strategic sales promotions.

Marketing hires

When we first started paying for marketing at Monday, I was pretty much our one-woman marketing department. That'll happen when you start your business – you wake up one day to find that you are the marketing department and the IT department and the HR department and the finance department. If you're lucky you'll share the load with another person or two, but it's very likely that you're something of a one-person circus act, juggling a million balls while riding on a unicycle just to stay upright.

Running a social media campaign isn't that hard to figure out, if you're willing to put in some research, which I was. Eventually Monday got big enough that I couldn't do it all myself – both because I had so much else to do and also because the marketing we needed went beyond my capabilities, or at least beyond my field of knowledge. I knew what we wanted, but I didn't necessarily know how to implement it all. By then we had enough money in the budget that we could pay someone to do our marketing, but we couldn't yet bring a marketing person – or, ideally, an entire marketing department – in-house, so we hired an external firm. Working with an agency was a huge learning experience for me. It had different representatives for every service – email marketing, Facebook marketing, SEO and overall strategy – so I learned from experts in each speciality. We learned that certain services were more important than others, which was great to know for down the road when we might hire in-house marketers. An agency is a good stopgap solution, because you gain the expertise of a firm that specialises in exactly what you need, but it can be costly. Not as costly as bringing on a full-time employee with benefits, maybe, but costly for a firm that will probably be splitting attention between you and other clients. Plus, it will charge you more for each additional piece you ask it to do – email, ads, SEO and so on. As soon as you can reasonably afford to bring someone in-house to run your company's marketing, do it. The minute I found the money in the budget for a full-time marketer, I was reaching out to potential candidates. Marketing is your company's portal to the world, so while it probably won't be the focus of the first person you hire (you need to actually have a product before you can ask someone to market the product), it should be a priority. Today Monday has a marketing department of eight people – some full-time and others freelance – and The Pilates Class has three marketers in-house as well.

The marketing calendar

Almost as important as where you roll out your marketing efforts is *when* you roll out your marketing efforts. When you launch a campaign, how often you promote, what time of day you post ... all of these factors will impact the effectiveness of your strategy. I know that social content often looks like it was posted on a whim, but here's a peek behind the curtain: if it looks that way it means the company is doing something right. It is creating content that's authentic to its brand and feels natural to its audience, and probably without the constant scramble to post the right thing at the right time, because doing that well takes time and forethought. Marketing content that is consistently high quality takes planning and preparation, just like everything in business.

From the earliest weeks of A Bikini A Day, before I could even articulate that what I was doing was marketing, I have lived by my companies' marketing calendars. At Monday we have two – nothing fancy or complicated, just simple Google Docs. The first covers our top-line strategy, basically a bird's-eye view of our biggest concepts of the year – launches, drops, events, collabs and more – that everyone in the company works from. (You can see an example of this in Appendix B.) A general rule of thumb is that you want to begin executing a marketing plan a minimum of three months in advance of whatever it is you're promoting, but I like to start strategising the marketing for any marquee moment at least six months before it happens. Again, that strategy will include all the various channels we're going to tap into, any events or press we might do, and any partnerships or cross-promotion we might engage in to build buzz. Then we have a second calendar that is entirely for social media, which outlines what we will post on each channel and when, down to the hour.

It might seem obsessive to be so granular about every little piece of social content or marketing content, but, first of all, if we know anything by now it's that being obsessed is part of the job description. But also, these details matter! There are so many analytics available these days that can tell you when your users are most engaged, so to ignore the information that is available to you would just be irresponsible. At Monday, we do all our product launches on Sunday, Monday and Wednesday. Part of that is based on when we know our customers are most likely to hit the 'buy now' button. Part of it is based on the fact that we're a company called Monday – there's some fun to launching on a Monday, and it offers a lot of creative opportunities. Like I said in the previous section, you need to work with the data you have, but allow yourself some creativity around it. Luckily, Mondays are generally a good time for posting on social anyway – people are back at work and in front of their computers, but they aren't necessarily in that nose-to-the-grindstone mentality just yet. Every company's user behaviour will be different, and honestly, if you research the 'best time to post on social media', every site might tell you something different, so the best thing you can do is gather your data and study your user. It does seem to be universally accepted that the worst day to post is Saturday, which makes sense, so don't bother doing any major promotion that day.

This may seem obvious, but it bears mentioning because

I've seen it go wrong: don't forget about time zones. The majority of my customers across both my businesses – probably 70 per cent of my total customers – are in the US. That means my marketing calendar is centred around the US time zones. Australia, for example, is anywhere from twelve to eighteen hours ahead of the US, depending on which areas of each country we're talking about, but we exclusively post based on what time it is in the States. If our primary customer base was in Australia or the UK, obviously that would be different. When we launched The Pilates Class during Covid, Jacqui and I were based in Australia and her regular clients at the studios where she worked were all based in Sydney, but we were trying to gain a bigger market share in the US and make that our target market so, again, I had to stress the importance of being on the US clock. Mentally, your marketing team needs to be wherever your customer is, even if you aren't there physically. (Don't worry – there are plenty of content management systems that allow you to schedule social posts to go live at a certain time – no one is asking you to stay awake until 3 a.m. so you can go live at the right time in a particular country on the other side of the globe).

Creating a calendar from day one of your business, when you don't have as much to talk about or promote, will help you tremendously in the future, when you feel like you can't fit one more thing into your marketing plan even if you tried. That's when you will most need to feel prepared and organised and like you've got things under control, and everything's a lot easier if you operate that way from day one. I love looking at the ways our marketing calendars have changed over time. If you build in structure from the start, you'll have a system in place if and when things get chaotic.

Ultimately, a marketing calendar is a framework. It is a guide that will help you look at your marketing plans as a whole and see how they all work together. Without one it is remarkably easy to lose the narrative thread – you throw out a bunch of content or ads or marketing materials, but they can feel fragmented. What you want is a cohesive whole – that's what distinguishes a marketing campaign from just a bunch of content. I often say that at Monday the marketing calendars are the most important documents in the company. We live in a world where content is king, so you need to be creating as much as you can. But if that content isn't rolled out strategically, in a way that is meaningful to your users, it loses its value. If that sounds stressful, start smaller. You should absolutely do less, but do it right, rather than go overboard with the content but with a half-ass launch. There are people out there who think that marketing is an afterthought – that a great product will simply market itself – but remember that nothing in a successful business 'just happens'. Every piece of the puzzle is thought out, and that's what makes it work.

10

Social media, the great equaliser

You are what you share.

CHARLES LEADBEATER

Social media has profoundly changed the ways companies market their products. Not only does it provide an opportunity for any company, with any budget, to quickly get into the marketing game, but it has made two-way communication between a brand and its audience much easier and more immediate. Users can provide instant feedback that can be collected in real time, and companies can develop relationships with their most loyal customers, capitalising on their dedication with ambassador or super-user programmes that benefit both parties equally. The possibilities for marketing with social media really do seem to be endless, and I feel quite confident in saying that, at the time of writing, we haven't seen even close to all of what social media has to offer the marketing world. After all, it's still so new. Facebook didn't launch until 2004. Instagram launched in 2010. TikTok launched in 2016. Threads launched in the summer of 2023, reportedly signing up one hundred million users in less than five days. Who knows what will come next? Not to mention the many sites that had a major moment and are now a relic of the past – MySpace, Friendster, Vine . . . remember them?

Consider, in comparison, that the world's first TV commercial aired in 1941. Newspaper ads started in the 1700s! Social media is in its infancy, and it's still growing at a rapid rate. And that's great news, not only because it offers opportunities for creativity and learning on a fairly equal playing field but also because you can reach an ever-growing audience. You have the opportunity to market your brand to the masses, and there will always be someone out there who resonates with what you have to say.

Before we dive into how to use social media to your advantage, it's worth understanding just how powerful this space is. Consider the following statistics:

- In 2023, nearly 4.9 billion people worldwide used social media. That's more than 60 per cent of the world population. ('50+ of the most important social media marketing statistics for 2023', *SproutSocial*)
- On a global scale, the average social media user has about eight social media accounts. ('Social network usage & growth statistics: How many people use social media in 2023?', *BackLinko*)
- The average user spends around 150 minutes a day on social media. ('50+ of the most important social media marketing statistics for 2023', *SproutSocial*)
- More than half of social media users (about 54 per cent) are women. ('Social Media demographics to inform your brand's strategy', *SproutSocial*)
- About 90 per cent of social media users follow at least

one brand. ('Top social media statistics and trends of 2023, *Forbes)*

- Social commerce – when customers shop directly from a social media platform – is growing. Experts predict it will grow to more than $2 trillion worldwide by 2025. ('Social commerce: The future of how consumers interact with brands', McKinsey & Company, 2022)

Bottom line: if you're just starting out, and you need to pick one area of marketing on which to focus your efforts and education, social media is it.

Start with the lowest-cost options

When you are launching a brand-new business, your marketing budget is likely to start out small, because your overall budget will probably be small, but don't let that deter you from diving into your social feeds from the start. Ideally, you want to start building your audience long before you actually launch your product so that there are people paying attention when your product or service actually drops.

Don't let the task of creating a following out of nothing scare you. Like any daunting business task, it's a matter of one step at a time. To start, create your social media handles. As is the case with your website URL, claim whatever name you can that is simple and straightforward and as similar to your business name as possible. If you can't get your exact business name, maybe you can add the word 'shop' in front if you sell goods, or something like 'we are' if you're a service. I don't like using characters like underscores or periods in my social media handles, because it's not as intuitive. This is not the place to be clever – just make it easy for customers to find you.

Next, make sure you fill out your full profile on each platform. There will be different fields depending on where you're posting, but again, the goal is to make it as easy as possible for customers to figure out where to find you and what you do. Include links, a description of your company, a hashtag or two if they are important to you, and the category your business falls into. I know this sounds obvious, but sometimes businesses are so focused on being innovative and creative that they forget to tackle the easy stuff, and users who haven't heard of you will consult these bios. They aren't just a formality. Remember that you don't have a lot of space to communicate everything you want your users to know. And the amount of space will change according to the platform. For example, on Insta, our Monday bio reads: 'Swimwear that takes you somewhere. Fits A–G cup sizes. Eco-friendly. We ship worldwide. Designed and tested by women for women.' On TikTok, by necessity, it's shorter: 'Swimwear that takes you somewhere. Fits A–G cup sizes. Eco-friendly.' Our bios for The Pilates Class are a bit more action oriented: 'One class, every "body"! Online Pilates Classes ♡ Healthy Recipes. FREE trial below!' On TikTok, we've whittled it down: 'Online Pilates Classes. By Jacqui Kingswell. FREE trial below👇'. The common thread in all these bios is that they focus on providing the customer with the most critical information *to them*: do they have my size? Do they have classes that fit my schedule? Will they ship to me? Can I do a trial class? With only a few sentences, we've used our social media platforms to deliver the important info about who we are, and how we can help our customer. That's no small thing.

The single best thing you can do in terms of generating free social media marketing is to create engaging posts. Content really is king and growing your audience is all about consistency. If you want to have a viral social media account or build an audience overnight you will need to make content creation a main focus for your business and your team. On Monday's Instagram account, we post three to five times per day on our grid and two to fifteen times a day on our Stories. Not to mention the content that goes up on all the other platforms. If you launch a business that relies heavily on social media to make sales, get ready to run on a hamster wheel. We create beautiful campaigns in some of the most exotic places in the world, constantly film video content, and post imagery from events or try-on hauls, but from one day to the next they move down the feed, sometimes never to be seen again. There are moments when it makes me sad that we don't celebrate the content that requires so much work – at least not the way we did when it was, say, printed in a magazine – but luckily I genuinely enjoy creating content. If you want to build similar businesses that require constant content, you'd better hope it's something you love and enjoy. Depending on the social platform, your content might include posts like we had at A Bikini A Day, which were visually appealing, or short videos highlighting a range of products or services. Interactive content – stuff like polls and surveys and AMAs (ask me anything) and quizzes – are always fun. Maybe you post behind-the-scenes content that shows what life at your company is like. It might feature an interview with you, the business owner, or give a peek at the offices or the making of your product. Giving users an inside look at your company helps you establish what your brand stands for and communicate whatever values are important to you. Maybe your differentiating factor is about community, or sustainability, or inclusiveness, or affordability. Letting users see who you are, especially at this time when consumers want to know *who* they are supporting with their spending, can be very impactful, and if your story resonates, users will share.

Low-cost marketing could also include offering discount codes to users, or running a contest or giveaway. If you allow people to enter only by 'tagging two friends', for example, you've basically built in a referral programme that will only cost you the price of whatever product you decide to give away. Referral programmes might also include giving early customers a code to share with friends, and giving the referrer a discount on their next purchase every time someone uses their code. Each of these approaches will cost you something in terms of sacrificing a full sale every now and then, but it's far cheaper than paying an outside marketing firm. You might also decide to partner with other small businesses for a cross-promotion or collaboration, so you each get exposure to the other business's audience. There is a wide range of options, all of which can be effective. More important than which route you choose is simply that you go in strategically – posting interesting content consistently, so that you begin to establish yourself.

The power of family and friends

It would be unfair and unreasonable of me not to at least acknowledge the fact that when Devin and I launched Monday, we already had a strong social media following. We were making a living as influencers, which meant we each already had the attention of tens of thousands of people. I'd be lying if I pretended that didn't make it easier for us to get our business off the ground and in front of a broad audience. I'm not sure we would have been able to take an entirely direct-to-consumer (DTC) route if we weren't able to plug into an existing audience early on and get them excited about the brand. If you already have a strong audience – from your own influencing or a previous business or a post that went viral and gained you lots of followers ... great. Use that. But if you don't, not to worry.

How many followers do you have on your various social media platforms, right this second? And how many followers does each of them have? It's quite likely that when you add it all up, that number is in the thousands, maybe even the tens of thousands. That's a pretty wide reach, and if you are someone who is starting a brand-new company, you should absolutely tap into it.

People underestimate the role of family and friends when it comes to launching a brand. These are people who should want to support you and see you do well. Don't be afraid to ask them for help. Start by reaching out to every friend and family member and telling them, 'I'm launching a business, can you please like and comment on every post I ever publish?' Ask them to share your posts too, so that their followers become your followers. I know it all sounds like a lot to ask, but it literally takes less than a second for someone to hit the like button or the heart or whatever that platform's equivalent is. Your friends don't have to leave long and insightful comments – a simple 'Amazing!' or 'I love this' or 'Can't wait to get mine!' goes a long way. If you're worried about looking desperate or that your friends will find this request annoying for whatever reason, explain to them that you're not just asking for this as an ego boost. The more engagement your posts get, and comments especially, the more people will see your post. It's an algorithm thing, but the gist is that comments are a signal to the social media platform that users find your posts interesting, which in turn signals to the platform that, *Hey, we should put this in front of more people.* As I mentioned, the goal of the algorithm is to serve people content that they want to see. If you post a piece of content that no one engages with, that's a signal that it's not very interesting, or that people don't care. If the first people who see a post don't care about it, the logical conclusion – at least to a social media algorithm – is that the next people won't either. But the opposite is also true: if lots of people care, then it stands to reason that even *more* people will care, if only they see it. When you ask your friends and family to comment, you are asking them to increase engagement on your post, because strong posts have a snowball effect. They just keep getting bigger and bigger as they pick up momentum.

Once you've asked your closest family and friends to follow your new accounts and share or engage with your content, ask your followers as a group. If, until now, all your social media accounts have been personal ones, then ostensibly everyone who follows you knows you in some way. Yes, it's possible they sat next to you in fifth grade and you haven't seen them since. But still, they are following you for a reason, and you never know what long-lost cousin is going to be the person who is happy to share your new venture and send you lots of potential customers. You could offer a 'friends and family' referral link in those early days, so that those who share your accounts and drive followers are somehow incentivised, but it's also possible that an honest, authentic ask can go a long way. Maybe you post something to your, say, four hundred followers that says something like: 'I'm so excited that I'm launching this business, it's been my entire focus for the last six months and an idea I've been obsessing about for years before that! It would mean so much to me if you would share this post with your followers, because I want to build an audience before I launch. I'm excited to share my passion with as many people as possible, and truly appreciate all the help I can get.' I think you'd be surprised at how willing people are to take this one small action. Honestly, people love helping someone out and being a part of a movement, as long as it's something they believe in or for someone they care about.

Which comes first?

It can feel like a bit of a chicken-and-egg conundrum: you need a social following in order to launch a product, but you need a product in order to build a social following. But rather than throw your hands up at the seeming impossibility of it all, remember what we've already covered. Even if you have only one hundred followers, that's so much better than starting with an audience of zero. Each of those one hundred people is a potential customer, and the source of information that can inform your business decisions.

I had a friend who wanted to start a business and felt completely daunted by the audience-building requirement, but then she had the idea to do an in-person event related to her product, with a panel of specialists, which I thought was totally clever. Let's say your product is for new moms, so you hold a panel discussion that includes a paediatrician, a preschool teacher and a psychologist. You invite every new mom you know, and tell them to invite their friends, and at the beginning you mention your upcoming launch and share your social handles. It's basically real-life community-building so that when the time comes, you have an audience to push your product out to. You could spend years building an audience if you're not quite ready to develop your product, and you'll be better off for it. That's what we did at Monday and it paid off big time.

Once you have your audience, not only can you ask them to share your content, but you can also prompt these people to sign up for more information (translation: your email list) so they will be the 'first to know' and 'have early access' when your products drop (everyone loves a sense of urgency and air of exclusivity). This database can help you learn about your customers. It can help you gauge interest in specific products, which in turn can help you figure out how much to order when you're just getting started. This is more important than you might initially realise. Remember our hiccup with the A Bikini A Day calendars? Let's say you're starting a company for fashionable snowsuits. Once you have the snowsuit designed, you need to get it made, which will involve placing an order with the manufacturer. That manufacturer, or supplier, will probably provide you with what's referred to as an MOQ, or minimum order quantity. This is what it sounds like: the minimum amount of stock you must order for a supplier to be willing to fill that order. This can be a tricky piece of the puzzle – you don't want to end up with a garage full of snowsuits if the MOQ is a thousand units and you expect that you can only, right now, sell a hundred. This is where your audience comes in: if you take pre-orders you can gauge the number of units you need to order. Maybe you realise that you need to put off your actual product drop until you can grow the customer base. Maybe you can incentivise the purchase of multiple items by offering free shipping if people spend over a certain threshold. Or maybe you discover that the excitement around your product is so major that you need to order more than the MOQ in order to keep up with demand.

All of this is really valuable information, so it's almost never too soon to start your social. If it's early enough that you don't yet have products to show, you can build excitement by doing a slow reveal of your branding (see the sample branding doc in Appendix D to get started) or posting photos that capture your aesthetic. For our snowsuit example, if your suits are high end and you are trying to attract the glamorous set, maybe you start by posting images of Telluride, Colorado, and St Moritz, Switzerland. Gorgeous images of the most luxurious snow getaways will start to associate your brand with these kinds of settings. If your snowsuits are more high intensity or extreme sports oriented, on the other hand, maybe you post images from the top of a double black diamond ski slope or a mountain known for its thrilling snowboard terrain. You can begin to create associations and set the tone for your brand on social before you've even introduced your user to any specific product.

Gathering feedback

Social media is a two-way street. You can speak directly to your customers, but your customers can also speak directly to you. Once upon a time, feedback was sent to a business via snail mail in a comment card, or maybe you would call a customer service hotline and wait on hold for an hour just to get a person on the other end of the phone. Today, customers might tweet a complaint or post on a brand's Facebook page, and their expectations for attention are quite high. According to an April 2022 report from the global management consulting firm McKinsey, 79 per cent of consumers expect a brand to respond to their questions or complaints via social within twenty-four hours. A full 40 per cent expect an answer within one hour. This same report found that only 50 per cent of companies actually meet those expectations. But for those who can, there's a big pay-off. American Express's 2017 Customer Service Barometer study found that 69 per cent of customers said they will spend more with a company that has good customer service; 90 per cent said they will tell other people when they have a good customer service experience, while 53 per cent said they will post online about their good customer service experiences. On the flip side, 33 per cent of customers will consider leaving a company immediately after a single instance of poor customer service, and 35 per cent will post online about that bad experience.

Handling customer service enquiries well on social media is important because, well, social media is a public forum. If you ignore a complaint or respond with something snarky, anyone can see it. And the last thing you want is to go viral for a customer service snafu. Customer service can directly affect brand reputation, and brand reputation is a key element of marketing. Make sure to take social media feedback from customers seriously, regardless of whether it's positive or negative. If you notice that you repeatedly get similar customer enquiries, post an FAQ to get ahead of it. Reply to all public feedback, if you can. And if you can't do so immediately, let your customers know the time frame in which they can expect a response. If the conversation is getting heated or complicated, take it to DM.

You also want to stay consistent to your brand – responses to customers, while always respectful, should sound like they are coming from your company, not a robot. Remember, this is a marketing moment, and you always want to stay true to your voice. If you do this well, you have the power to turn negative feedback into a positive experience. Customers who complain but then get the helpful response they're looking for, quickly, can be converted into your greatest fans.

At The Pilates Class, because it's a global community, we also use social media to gather customer feedback via WhatsApp focus groups. We have chats on the app with the most loyal members of the TPC community for many major cities across the globe – Sydney, London, New York,

LA – and we even ask the most passionate ambassadors to step up as leaders in their areas, organising meetups and helping to take the TPC brand offline and into real life. These microcommunities become sources for market research, and they allow the TPC team to get to know our users in different communities without the added expense of making our employees travel across the world. Perhaps, for your business, a different platform will make more sense. With Monday, for example we send our customers quarterly questionnaires via email. But if you have a global market, social media is a great way to connect with customers across different cities to learn more about their needs and what resonates with them.

Creating a successful social launch

Let's say you've built your social audience. You've used it to build brand loyalty and establish your reputation and get a sense of your numbers in terms of minimum orders. Now it's time to launch. Maybe you're launching the whole business, maybe you're launching a new line or collection or an updated model of a classic product. It doesn't particularly matter in this case, because the reality is that you should make a big deal out of it no matter what you are launching. Make it seem like it's something major, with a lot of fanfare in the lead-up, a splashy drop and constant hoopla in the first week. If you don't have the bandwidth to do all that, then you shouldn't launch at all. And I'm not just saying that. At Monday, 90 per cent of our sales for any new colour or collection happen in the first week. If we realise that we are stretched too thin that week, or if it's a holiday where our users will be distracted and we won't have their usual attention, we delay. It's simply not worth sacrificing the first week of sales, or half-assing the first week of promotion.

Keep in mind that I say this as the owner of a company that launches a new colour or style *every single week*. We do everything in our power to launch every single one on social with a giant splash. We tease the lead-up, then promote the launch, then we highlight any advertisements, then re-share the influencers who are talking about the launch on their channels. At Monday, this usually starts with an email to customers, then Devin and I do posts on our personal social accounts, and then we have one on the Monday account, and then we start showcasing the influencers (paid and not) and users who have tried it. The content of these posts is usually pretty obvious – it's all about the product. It's generally as easy as, 'We have a new collection, look how beautiful it is, here's a link to the shop.'

At The Pilates Class, we don't always have something tactile to show off, so we have to be a bit more thoughtful. When we have, say, a new weekly workout online, we'll share a video from the instructor explaining what to expect, a clip of the workout itself, a clip of Jacqui promoting the workout, and we'll even create a graphic of the positive feedback on the workout and share that as a video scroll or a photo. We often intersperse these class promotions with drops of new recipes or cookbooks or challenges or fitness guides, because these kinds of initiatives help generate excitement and retain interest. But no matter what we're launching, the question is always the same: 'What three or four things are we going to do in week one to capitalise on this launch?' If it's a cookbook, maybe I want a Live of someone making the recipe, and I want to share a pic of someone who made this at home, and I want beautiful photographs of the finished meal, and I want an easy ingredients-list graphic for our users' shopping lists.

Doing all this goes back to that rule of seven and the importance of getting your product in front of a potential customer multiple times if you want to secure a sale. What's funny is that even as a business owner myself, and someone who absolutely knows the power of marketing and how it weasels its way into our psyche, I'm still as affected as anyone. I'll see a designer launch a bag and I'll think to myself, *That's not really that cute.* Then I start to notice it popping up in my social feeds and printed on billboards. Then I see a really fashionable person wearing it, styled in a really cute way. Suddenly it's in my cart, and I don't know what happened! The psychology is real: your user sees something once, they might think, *Oh, I like that,* and go on with their day. Seven or eight times later, they're suddenly thinking, *I really do like that dress, and I could probably wear it to that wedding next month.* Congratulations, you just made a sale.

As you can tell, there's a lot to keep track of when it comes to launching a brand on social media. But I want it to be as easy for you as possible! Here's what you need to know:

My top ten tips to building a successful social launch

1. Start your social accounts long before you launch your products.
2. Choose the two or three social channels that make the most sense for your brand.

3. Write a company bio that is short and easy to understand, which also gives the important info about your company.

4. Create engaging content. Think beautiful images, behind-the-scenes videos, polls, AMAs. If you don't have any products to show yet, do a slow branding reveal, or post images with a similar aesthetic or that would appeal to your customer base.

5. Know your brand voice and use it always.

6. Tap into family and friends. Ask them to like, comment, share and repost.

7. Encourage your followers to sign up for early access – this will mean getting their email addresses.

8. Respond to customer feedback on social media quickly and respectfully.

9. Be strategic about when you launch and post. Audience analytics tools can tell you when your followers are most engaged – schedule your launch accordingly.

10. Make a big deal of your launch ... because it *is* a big deal! You should be posting many times a day in the lead-up to the launch, on the day of the launch and in the immediate aftermath.

The face of your brand

Before you finalise your social media marketing plans, you need to ask yourself one last question: 'Will you be the face of your brand?' Some people love being in front of the camera, others hate it, but your decision should take into account more than just your desire to be in an ad or on a billboard.

Personally, I prefer to own brands that have a 'face' attached, because it feels more meaningful to me. That said, it's not always appropriate or necessary. First, consider the type of business you are starting. Some lend themselves to needing a 'face' more than others. Fashion and beauty brands are conducive to having a personality who represents the business because that person can wear the clothing or jewellery or make-up they are selling and show them off in marketing materials. It's a more natural inclusion of a specific face than, say, a dishware company. That said, people use products, so this alone shouldn't dictate your decision – there's an organic way to include your spokesperson no matter your product if that's a necessary part of your branding.

Are you a recognisable face? Do you already have a strong following? If you are someone with notoriety, and a generally positive reputation, being associated with your brand can help boost sales. If people feel like they know you, they may want to support you. Or maybe they are a fan, so by proxy they're a fan of whatever you associate yourself with.

It's also worth considering that customers connect more to a brand when it is connected to a personality. Consumers want to see that there is a human behind the companies they support. Of course, the human in question doesn't have to be you. If you hire social media managers who are happy to answer questions on social or talk to your users, that might be enough. But the argument that it *should* be you is simple: you are the expert on your company, you are the person who is excessively obsessed, you are the one who can speak to the company's very beginnings, to how you came up with the idea and why it's needed. If your passion is infectious, there's a strong case to be made that you should be out there to pass it on to others.

As you're considering this decision, keep in mind that the future is always uncertain. Being the face of your brand might make a ton of sense now, but what might it mean in the future? What if you sell your company one day; what will your obligations be? If that's your ultimate end goal, you may not want to be so intimately linked to your company's branding – that way, separation can be less obvious and more low profile when the time comes. You won't have to create a new brand identity. Devin and I are absolutely the faces of Monday, but at this point we've built the brand enough that if we needed to step away for any reason, it has a loyal customer base and following independent of us. Still, it would be noticeable, and if that worries you, you may not want to be your brand representative.

Being the face of the company also forces you to care about the business even more than you already do. I know that sounds strange – this is your baby! You're obsessed with it! I get that. But if your face is attached to your brand, you will feel even more responsible for it, because people will absolutely expect you to answer for anything that goes wrong. I certainly find that our competitor brands with no 'face' are held less accountable than we are, but I like to see that as an advantage. Being held to a higher standard means you'll have no choice other than to meet that higher standard, and that's a positive. Still, like everything in business, choosing to put your image on your marketing materials is complicated. If there's one lesson in business, perhaps that's it: nothing is ever as easy as it seems.

PART 4

Finding fulfilment, avoiding burnout

11

Your wellness is your business's biggest asset

The most important investment you can make is in yourself.

WARREN BUFFETT

When you first launch a company, that business will be your baby. You will love it and nurture it and think about it constantly. But you know how they tell parents on an aeroplane to 'put your oxygen mask on first'? That rule applies here too. Doing anything to the point of excess comes with risks, and obsessing about your business is no different. Yes, you eat, sleep and breathe work in your earliest days of entrepreneurism, but you won't win any medals for working yourself to the point of sheer exhaustion. Despite what #hustleculture might have you believe, surviving on zero sleep is nothing to brag about. There was a time when pointing out on social media that you hadn't taken a day off in a month was seen as something of a humblebrag – especially for women in business – because, supposedly, it meant you were killing it at work and there was some honour in sacrificing your personal joy for the sake of professional success. The #girlboss movement sent the message that the path to success was as easy as spending every second of your life in pursuit of success. (No big deal, right?) But the good news is, those days are over. That sort of existence isn't sustainable – and the burnout that results is very real. To be a business owner with a chance at longevity (the ultimate goal), what you need is balance.

Burnout is real

For as long as I can remember, and certainly for as long as I've been a business owner, I've been the kind of person who jumps out of bed on a Monday morning excited to tackle the day and conquer the world. Having a sense of purpose and drive and fulfilment from what you do can be addictive, and it's easy to roll your eyes at the people who tell you to take care of yourself first, or to take a mental health day. *You don't know what it's like*, you might think to yourself. *That's such a hippy-dippy idea*, you might say when they aren't listening. (I certainly did.) You might be like me and think that you thrive in a 'hustle' state, which makes it feel natural, rather than like something that could work against you. But working, working, working, with hardly any downtime, can have extreme negative effects – and they can sneak up on you with no warning.

In June of 2022, I developed a bad case of Covid, which for me included tension headaches, extreme fatigue, dizziness, joint and muscle pain, and brain fog. The symptoms lasted for months, eventually improving and then regressing nearly overnight. Eventually I was diagnosed with long Covid. For a while I could barely walk. I certainly couldn't exercise or work for hours on end, and I developed some real anxiety around my inability to be productive. At one point, I had to be taken off a flight because of severe muscle pain and an irregular heartbeat. It was crippling – I'm an active person, and I live for my work and my fitness – but I was certainly not the only one going through that same suffering. Women outnumber men four to one when it comes to developing long Covid, and it specifically affects healthy, active women. I can't say exactly why this happened to me – I'm not a doctor, and there are still plenty of questions around Covid and the way it affects people – but I'm confident that the fact that my body was running on empty didn't help. At the time that I first caught Covid, I was deeply involved in three different businesses and I wasn't taking much (or really any) time for rest. I *thought* I rested, because I got eight hours of sleep each night and had the occasional massage, but I was the kind of person who would get her wisdom teeth out and then go straight from the dentist's office to the computer, and I was proud of that. I was constantly busy and I fuelled myself with adrenaline rather than taking the time to nourish myself with sleep or focus on my mental health.

Looking back, it's almost laughable – when I was in the throes of that constant work, I thought I was so fit and strong. I worked out a lot, I felt great about the way I looked, I was killing it at work. But I had no balance and there were warning signs I ignored. During the pandemic, I didn't use the time to slow down or take time off – I hustled ten times harder. I was working with teams across the globe and my hours were 7 a.m. to 7 p.m. Whenever I wasn't at my desk, I was working on my phone. My headaches were getting worse and worse, my neck pain was at an all-time high and my eyesight was going downhill fast, and still I was addicted. I had all the drive and all the *doing* without any of the rest and recovery. One of the problems with living this way is that you don't necessarily realise how bad it is for you until things take a serious turn for the worse. I was moving at such a fast pace and things were going so well that I thought I had everything figured out. In reality, my body could only handle the relentless pace of my professional life because it didn't have anything else to contend with. The minute there was a physical challenge in addition to the mental challenge of running multiple businesses, my body said, *no thanks.* In the moments when you *think* you can do it all, you will be even more surprised when something comes and takes you out. Every person, and every body, has a limit and if you use up all its strength and power on work, there's nothing left to fight illnesses or disease. If it wasn't Covid that sidelined me I think it would have been something else. My inner voice knew I needed to slow down, but it was my head vs my heart, so I ignored the warning signs I would normally have been so in tune with.

My experience with long Covid is an extreme example of the physical effects of imbalance, and I hope something similar never happens to you. But burnout comes for all of us if we subscribe to hustle culture at the expense of taking care of ourselves. What is burnout, exactly? It can feel like one of those 'you know it when you feel it' maladies, that specific form of exhaustion that comes from constantly feeling swamped, like there's so much to do and never enough time and you simply have to keep going with no rest. It's a common enough phenomenon that the World Health Organization even defined it in its eleventh revision of the International Classification of Diseases: 'Burn-out is a syndrome conceptualized as resulting from chronic workplace stress that has not been successfully managed.' It is characterised by 'feelings of energy depletion or exhaustion', among other things. According to a 2016 survey of 326 entrepreneurs published in the *Journal of Small Business Management* and reported on in *Harvard Business Review*, while the average entrepreneur in the survey said they experienced some burnout, 25 per cent said they were moderately burned out, and 3 per cent said they were strongly burned out. And the health effects of burnout are real. It can lead to excessive stress, heart disease, high blood pressure, insomnia, and more ... including an increased vulnerability to illness, according to the Mayo Clinic, a US hospital ranked number one in *Newsweek's* list of top hospitals worldwide in 2023.

Imagine standing on a balance beam. If you are leaning all the way to one side, tipping over rather than firmly planted, the moment something tries to knock you over you'll probably go down quickly. But if you're steady and centred, the same disturbance that might make someone else fall will merely give you a wobble. That's why balance is so critical. As a business owner, you will be busy. It comes with the territory. But if you know that and you prepare for it, and implement strategies to take care of yourself, you can arm yourself with the tools to handle the stress. That might mean scheduling a weekly appointment with a therapist, or blocking off time in your calendar for rest or relaxation a couple of afternoons a week. It might mean making a regular weekly lunch date with a friend, or carving out time to meditate each morning. Most successful entrepreneurs I know have had to learn this the hard way, finding themselves in a moment that feels like a breakdown, whether it was a physical illness or suffering so much stress it borders on a panic attack. When that happens, you can only hope it isn't too late – that you can take the rest and recovery you need and rely on your team to keep the ship afloat while you do so. A much better option is to understand the risks of burnout, know you aren't immune to it (no one is) and do what you can now to prevent it from coming for you later.

Healthy you, healthy company

Protecting and retaining your good health is hopefully reason enough for you to build a little balance into your life. But if not, consider this: your health and wellness isn't just about keeping you in good shape. It's also critical to keeping your business up and running.

There are so many reasons why your personal health will affect your professional business. Let's start with the obvious. In the beginning, your business might be just you, or you and a business partner, or you and a handful of employees. There will come a time when your company will operate like a well-oiled machine, and you can call in sick or take a vacation and operations will continue without anyone even noticing your absence. In fact, in my opinion, a defining characteristic of a leader is not that their company can't survive without them, but that it *can*. If you've trained your team well enough, and put enough effective systems in place that the company can operate without your constant presence, consider your job well done. But getting to that point takes time, and when your business is just getting off the ground, your presence will be very necessary. You might even be the only employee – which means you *are* the business. Or you might be the information hub, the only person involved who knows all the little details – or even the big ones – that keep operations moving forwards. Questions like 'What deadline did we give the manufacturer?' or 'How much did we decide to charge for shipping?' or 'What was the deal we negotiated with the web designer?' ... It's likely that you are the repository for all that information.

You're also probably the visionary and the decision-maker. If you're the person who came up with the business idea, only you will know how exactly you want your product to look or how you want to structure your different service packages. There are so many important decisions made in the early days, and if you're not available to make them, well, two things could happen. They could stall, delaying your progress or your launch date, or someone else will make the decisions, and maybe you'll agree with them, and maybe you won't. If you're running a business that you conceived, then I'm guessing you'll want certain things done your way. At the very least, you'll want to weigh in on important decisions, and to do so you need to be present. This doesn't mean you can't take a day off once in a while, of course, but it means you need to be well enough to weigh in on decisions and come to them with a clear mind. If you are a one- or even two-person business and you are suddenly out of commission, your business could be too.

Speaking of a clear mind, there's more than just stress or physical illness that can mess with your decision-making skills. I rarely drink and have never done drugs. That may sound boring, but I can't afford to indulge in substances that will hamper my ability to think clearly. My business relies on my ability to weigh options and make smart choices and avoid impulsiveness or brain fog, but in addition to my duties as decision-maker, I take my responsibilities as a leader and manager very seriously. It's not just my own job that's at risk if I'm not performing at the top of my game – I have teams who rely on my leadership and employees who rely on our company to deliver their steady pay cheque. The fact that other people's livelihoods are dependent on my ability to think strategically and lead a company to success is not lost on me for a single second. The only way to make balanced decisions is to be a balanced person.

TIPS FOR AVOIDING BURNOUT

At home

- **Get enough sleep.** According to a 2019 study of more than 11,000 adults across twelve countries, the average adult gets only 6.8 hours of sleep on weeknights (and 7.8 at weekends). The recommended amount? Eight hours. Try to make your bedroom a tech-free zone, and cut out screens from 8 p.m. onwards. (I charge my phone away from my bed so I'm not tempted!)

- **Move your body.** What you do will depend on your interests. I like Pilates (obviously) and going for walks. You might like running or dancing or yoga or swimming or lifting weights. What matters is that you get those endorphins flowing as these are the hormones that reduce stress and improve well-being. The truth for me is that work and fitness are my drugs – there's only one thing that compares to the feeling of starting a new project and it's the feeling of working out to my favourite playlist. It gets my heart pumping and puts a smile on my face every time!

- **Connect with friends.** Socialising isn't just fun, it has proven health benefits, including reducing stress and improving mental health. Spending time with those who know and love you outside of your work environment can also serve as a welcome reminder that you are more than your job, and that a world and support system exists for you outside your professional life.

- **Meditate and breathe.** Several studies have found that meditation can help prevent burnout. It doesn't need to take long, either. Ten minutes a day can make a big difference, but if five minutes is all you have, or sitting still is so hard for you that you have to start with two minutes, that's better than nothing. Women in particular are sensitive to adrenal highs. I used to run on adrenaline all the time, and for a while I thought I thrived in that state – until I learned you can only sustain that so long. Now, I feel very in tune with my body, so when I start to feel a bit edgy or when my body is in overdrive I use meditation and breathing techniques to settle myself (specifically my nervous system), at least temporarily.
- **Engage in an offline hobby.** Balance means finding something you care about and enjoy doing *aside* from working. When you are managing the stress and pressure of running a business, there's a lot of value in finding something you enjoy where you can lose yourself in the *doing* rather than worrying about a successful outcome.
- **Avoid unnecessary technology.** I used to wake up and check my emails before I was even out of bed. Then I was on my laptop all day and I'd wind down by watching TV at night. Translation: I was staring at a screen from dawn to dusk. Now I try to have dinner outside, or institute technology-free meals, holidays or even entire weekends. I even embrace chores like blowing the leaves and taking out the trash. Plus, I love cooking as a grounding activity that gets me away from technology.

- **Talk to a professional.** Running a business can be a lot of pressure – at times it can feel like the weight of the world is on your shoulders. A therapist or other mental health professional can help you manage the many ups and downs that come with the entrepreneurial lifestyle before the emotions get the better of you.

- **Spend time in nature.** Of all of these tips, this one is most important to me. We are confined to small spaces more than ever these days – chained to a desk, staring at screens for eight-plus hours a day – and connecting with nature is a way to ground yourself and connect more with the world around you. Whether it's taking a walk first thing in the morning to get sunlight on your face before you go online, or taking a break at lunch to walk barefoot at your local park, a moment outside will work wonders for your soul. I try to take a hike or an ocean swim, or just allow my eyes to look at what they are really made to look at . . . the world!

- **Be wary of toxic relationships.** Your personal relationships play a huge role when it comes to stress. You can't do it all – you cannot manage a stressful or toxic personal life and also put your all into a fully fledged business. This combination will run you ragged and it's not spoken about enough. There have been times when I've felt like I was just keeping my head above water in my personal life and no one would have known it at work. The office is my happy place, so when things have been hard at home or with family I just dive even deeper into my work. That isn't healthy. Make sure the people you spend the most time with uplift you, inspire you, and treat you with love and respect. Once you become successful, your personal relationships can change, so it's important to pay attention to who makes you feel happy in your downtime and who is draining your energy.

- **Create boundaries.** It's important to understand that it will be hard to balance 'it all' as a woman in business. Family commitments, a social life, perhaps maintaining a home: it all takes energy and time. Be gentle on yourself if you need to miss out on a cousin's birthday party or a friend's dinner party in order to preserve your mental health. And learn to say no. One of the biggest advantages I had when I started my businesses is that I had moved overseas. I didn't have all the family or friend commitments I normally would, and that allowed to me to focus all my time and energy on building my business. Of course I still came home to visit my family and spoke to them regularly, but it really took the pressure off. Not everyone can relate to or understand what it's like to run your own business and there will be people that think you've become 'selfish' for putting yourself first. But as I always say, 'those who get it, get it', and they're my type of people.

- **Manage stress.** It's easy to get caught up in the constant issues that arise in a business, going home to your partner and discussing that day's hiccups for hours on end or stressing out constantly more than you really have to. I like to think of life as the yin and the yang. This is something simple my dad taught me, and I think it's quite profound. Life has to be a balance of good and bad, it's just the way the energy of the world works. Ever noticed that whenever everything starts going so well for you . . . boom, another issue takes you back down? When that happens to me, which it does *a lot* and on a daily basis, I just smile and think of my dad. 'There it is, the balance of life.' Unless your health is affected there's really nothing in life that is worth stressing over. There is always a solution, it will always work out and you really have to believe that down to your core. Stress has been proven to cause illness, so try to take issues in business that aren't life altering with a grain of salt.

- **Slow down.** If there's anything I learned from my battle with long Covid it's that slow and steady wins the race. For me when I say slow, I just mean 'slow-*er*'. When I was sick, my doctor said to me one day, 'I bet you eat at your desk, or during meetings. I bet you're always rushing, even when you're going to the bathroom.' I'm a fast-paced person when it comes to my working day, constantly rushing and chasing a momentum, but it's not totally necessary. Now I slow down when I eat my food, I drive a bit slower, I just generally try to work on feeling more calm and relaxed throughout my day. And in the end, everything still gets done at the same time, but my energy is more balanced, I sit back in my chair more and my body is in a relaxed state. A lot of women are so used to doing it all and having no time in their day that they get stuck in a perpetual state of rushing. I'm proud to say I'm not in that state any more.

At work

- **Delegate.** Are there tasks you're in charge of that someone else could handle? Maybe you only do them because you've always done them, but now you can pass them off to another team member. Maybe you don't like to relinquish control. I get it. But you're only one person, and you can only do so much.
- **Get support.** Just because you're in charge doesn't mean you don't need help. Networking and support groups exist for CEOs and business leaders who want to trade ideas and discuss the challenges of running a business, but if you don't want to join a formal group, maybe you can organise a monthly lunch with other business owners you know. Or ask another entrepreneur out for coffee to swap stories and advice.
- **Use the 20/20 rule.** Nothing good ever came from sitting at a desk and staring at a screen for hours on end. I used to sit at my laptop for hours, even all day, without taking a break. Staring at the screen all day hurt my eyes – and sped up their overall decline – and for some it can cause migraines and neck pain, among other negative effects. I implemented the 20/20 rule later than I should have, but now I set

a timer on my phone to remind me, every twenty minutes, to step away from the computer for a minimum of twenty seconds. Maybe I get up and get water or go to the bathroom (you'd be surprised how often you forget to go when you're focused on work). Maybe I just do a quick stretch, stand up or close my eyes and breathe. I take that alarm very seriously – I'm always surprised when it goes off, and without it I know I would probably forget to take a break at all.

- **Take days off.** When you are launching a business, even weekends turn into workdays. But everyone needs a break now and then. You may not be able to take a week-long vacation, but the business should be able to spare you for a day or two, and you'd be surprised how effective even twenty-four hours of unplugging can be for refreshing your energy.

- **Have in-person meetings.** Zoom took over during the pandemic and I still believe it's an important work tool, but I like to hold internal team meetings in person as often as possible. Interacting with others in real life helps build stronger and more fulfilling connections.

- **Create an organisational system.** Managing tasks as they come up can feel like playing Whac-A-Mole: chaotic, with no predictability or moment of downtime. Creating a method for the madness will give you a sense of order and control. Choose whatever method works for you. Maybe you start the day with a 'power hour' during which you crank through as many tasks as possible before you jump into your meetings. Or perhaps you come up with a colour-coding system that indicates priority: red for urgent, yellow for medium priority (needs to be done in the next few days), green for long-term to-dos.

- **Eat (a nutritious) lunch away from the computer.** If nothing else, please avoid the desk lunch. First of all, eating a decent meal is imperative when it comes to nourishing your body and mind during the exhausting days of starting up a business. But eating at your desk has been shown to have all sorts of negative consequences: it usually leads to mindless eating (since you're focused on your screen instead of your food), it's bad for your posture and thus hard on your body, and it's isolating during a time that is ripe for social connection. You don't need to take a full hour, but give yourself fifteen minutes at least.

Culture starts at the top

As the leader of your company, you set the tone. The way you behave will establish what is expected of your team, and the culture in which you expect your employees or business partners to work. If you show up to the office, or the Zoom calls, in good spirits and with a positive, inspiring, can-do attitude, it will send the message to your employees that all is well. Yes, they need to work hard, but that's a lot easier to do in an environment where they are treated well. You will establish an overall sentiment of 'we are happy to be here'. Leadership is about setting a good example, so if you come to work as your best self, your employees will do the same. This is the beautiful thing about running a small business – the culture is something you have a strong influence over.

If, on the other hand, you show up oozing stress and exhaustion, that will be how your workers view the environment you've created. When asked about the vibe in their workplace, the employees at your company might describe it as chaotic or a rat race, a constant fight to keep their heads above water. Your stress might signal to your employees – accurately or not – that the business is struggling. When a leader seems on edge or tense, employees will often assume it's an indication that something is going wrong behind the scenes. From that assumption, they may begin to worry about their job security, which will put them on edge as well. Now you've got employees that are feeling stressed or burned out, which will mean they can't function at the top of their game or do their best work. It's a trickle-down effect, and it all starts with you.

Even if you think you do a great job of hiding your exhaustion or stress from your employees – if you never utter a word about not sleeping or being overworked or not having enough time for, well, anything – keep in mind that burnout is insidious and can affect how you treat others without you even realising it. If you aren't taking care of yourself, for example, you're much more likely to be short on patience. You might be quicker to snap at an employee who makes a mistake. You may just be less friendly and approachable, which could make workers worry that you don't like them or that they've done something wrong. Good leadership takes effort and energy, both of which can be in short supply when you aren't your best self.

For all the work you put into making sure you're taking care of yourself, keep in mind that it's just as important to have

employees who do the same. Sure, they probably (and hopefully) won't actually be as overworked as you are, because
they aren't running the entire business, but it's quite likely
that they may *feel* as overworked. As pretty much anyone who
has ever held a job knows, work can be stressful. I don't care
if you are the CEO or an assistant or an intern, if you care
about your work product it's easy to get caught up, checking
your work email from home or putting in extra hours at the
weekend. According to the Future Forum Pulse Report Fall
2022, a global survey of more than 10,000 workers across
Australia, France, Germany, Japan, the UK and the US, a
whopping 42 per cent of desk workers reported feeling burned
out. And aside from that feeling being problematic on an individual level, employees suffering burnout are simply bad for
business. Research shows that burned-out employees are less
productive, less innovative, less engaged and more likely to
make mistakes. And burnout is terrible for morale – it's hard
to be a positive and involved employee when you feel like you
are barely keeping it together. Burnout also leads to higher
employee turnover and increased risk of workplace absence.

So what can you do about it? As the business leader, it's
within your purview to organise (or empower someone on
your team to organise) morale-boosting events for your entire
organisation. Monday and The Pilates Class are both companies that encourage our customers to live their best lives
and be their best and most confident selves, so it's important
to me that we encourage our employees to do the same. At
The Pilates Class and The Birthing Class, we offer annual
mental health days so our employees can take a break to
relax and recharge. At Monday we regularly do team lunches
and recently we even brought in our campaign photographer
to do a super-chic studio shoot for our whole team – a fun
pick-me-up so that everyone who works for Monday could

take a break and have a little fun. At both companies we do 'team sweats', in which a trainer will come in and lead a group workout. We also invite team members to special brand events, even when they wouldn't normally get to be there, because we want everyone to feel the excitement of an important company accomplishment. Burnout is defined, in part, by feelings of cynicism, which can come from feeling like your work isn't actually *contributing* to anything, or that there's no point to whatever you are doing. Being present to see the exciting pay-off of your company's hard work can help keep those cynical feelings at bay.

Flexibility is key

In the post-pandemic world, flexibility in the office is highly valued. Employees expect to be able to work from home a couple of days a week, or at least to be able to call in remotely for meetings when necessary. But from the start, long before Covid, I set up all my companies so that I could work remotely. Not all businesses will allow for that of course – if you're a chef and restaurant owner you'll need to be present until you can train your sous chef to run the kitchen for you – but, if you can, build your business from day one so that it can operate without your physical presence. Yes, I believe in unplugging or taking a day off once in a while, but I also know the reality of running an early-stage business, and that means you may want to take a day off on the very same Tuesday that you're needed at a high-stakes client meeting. This shouldn't be an either/or – you don't have to choose between your day off and your meeting, as long as your business is set up so that you can participate remotely. Sure, calling into a meeting from a hotel is not the same level of relaxation as being completely out of office, but it's better than nothing. Every step you can take to preserve your mental health and institute some self-care will make a difference. It's not all or nothing.

Flexibility matters for your workers too. In fact, the same Future Forum global survey which discovered that more than 40 per cent of workers worldwide suffer from burnout also found that flexibility is the factor that could help reverse the trend. Employees who are unhappy with their flexibility options are 43 per cent more likely to say they're burned out than those who feel they have a good amount of flexibility. And that flexibility applies not only to *where* they work but also *when*. If you can offer your employees flexible schedules in terms of their specific working hours, it could go a long way towards keeping burnout from coming for your workforce.

At all of my companies, one of our most steadfast philosophies is to trust our team and give them independence. As business owners, we work with our employees closely in person when they're first hired, in order to be sure they're aligned with the company's expectations, but then we pretty much let them work on their own schedule and decide whether they want to be in the office or work from home, just like us! We all have the same mission: to see the brand do as well as possible. We trust that our employees always have the brand's best interests at heart. Of course, if we notice someone is falling behind or not working like they should we will discuss that with them individually – sometimes there's a reason that we can be compassionate about, other times there isn't. But we treat our team like family. After all, we're all human beings and require a certain level of trust and compassion to feel appreciated.

In the years since I was sidelined with Covid, I've changed the way I work. It was a pretty major wake-up call: I couldn't continue pushing at that same pace and expect my health to improve. Today, I mostly take all the advice I've laid out for you here. But we're all human, and those of us who are excessively obsessed can find ourselves fixating on work issues or getting swept up in a new idea, and losing the balance that we worked so hard to create. Hopefully over time you can learn the personal signs that you're imbalanced: disrupted sleep, anxious thoughts, a shorter temper. Maybe you haven't seen a friend in person in a month. Or maybe someone you love has mentioned how hard you're working, and they think you should take it easy. Maybe you're yawning all the time or getting more frequent headaches. Take all these as hints that it's time for a wellness check. Your body, and your business, will thank you.

12

You need alone time

*Almost everything will work again if you unplug it for
a few minutes, including you.*

ANNE LAMOTT

I love being alone. I'm a social being and absolutely adore
my girlfriends and my family and my co-workers, but it's
during moments of solitude that I have my best ideas or find
the energy to tackle complicated problems or ground myself
back to a place of balance. In fact, people often comment on
how lucky I am that I get to travel to beautiful far-off places
and spend time in exotic locales, and it's true, I love seeing
the world, but one of the best parts of travel, for me, is the
time in the air. Hours spent on a plane always feel like the
ideal window to reflect on my days, form my own opinions
on personal, professional and even global issues, and – simply
but most importantly – just breathe.

When your business gets to a place where you have a team
you're leading and partners you're collaborating with, or even
investors who have a stake in your financial outcomes, there
will always be people who need something from you. Your

business partner might need you to weigh in on strategic decisions about expansion. Employees may need you to offer guidance on upcoming campaigns or launches. Outside vendors will need approvals and payments. Investors will need updates on company progress. There could also be social accounts you need to appear on, journalists who are asking for interviews and customers who've reached out with service issues that have been bubbled up to the top. You may also need to interview potential new hires or let go of employees that aren't working out. There is truly no end to the demands on your time and energy and attention when you are running a business. Which is not to say that you should be giving of yourself constantly but that the only one who can really be trusted to protect your alone time is you. And when it feels like someone is always tugging at you for just one more thing, that alone time is even more precious, and even more important. You know those movies where the harried parents are constantly surrounded by chaos and then suddenly their kids go to camp or to the grandparents' house and the parents look at each other and say something like, 'Do you hear that? The sweet sound of silence?' (Or maybe you even know this from experience!) That's what it can feel like to run a business. Moments of quiet are blissful, and all too rare.

The creative connection

A lot of attention and lip service is paid to the notion of collaboration being important to creativity, and I know there's a lot to be gained by putting heads together. Two minds are better than one and all that. At my businesses, we know that great ideas can come from anyone and anywhere, and part of the reason we emphasise team-building is that we want employees to work together to solve problems or innovate. But solitude is also critical to creativity. Have you ever noticed that some of your best ideas come to you in the shower, when you're driving or going for a run, or even when you're washing the dishes? It's not just you. Researchers often refer to the 'shower effect' when talking about creativity – it's the outcome of letting your mind wander, which you can do when engaged in an activity where you don't need to fixate too much on whatever task you're performing in the moment. A 2019 study of ninety-eight writers and eighty-seven physicists, published in the journal *Psychological Science*, asked them to each record what they were doing when they had their most creative idea of the day; 20 per cent of the ideas occurred during 'spontaneous task-independent mind wandering' – in other words, while not at work, and not actually thinking about the idea or problem at hand – and these ideas were more likely to be considered 'aha moments' or associated with 'overcoming an impasse'. Other research has found that showering, exercising and being in transit are the activities most likely to spark moments of creativity.

Even if you aren't in a 'mind-wandering' place, research also shows that some of the best thinking is done in solitude. Group brainstorms are a common workplace activity, but brainstorming is actually more successful when it's done independently. Same with complicated problem-solving. As Steve Wozniak, co-founder of Apple, noted: 'I don't believe anything really revolutionary has ever been invented by committee.'

But the reverse is also true. As much as alone time is conducive to creativity, it's also the case that creative people are more likely to harness their alone time for brainstorming. A 2023 study published in the *Creativity Research Journal* found that creative people are more likely to make the most of idle time by letting their thoughts wander, and feel less bored when spending time alone.

When I talk about creatives, I'm not referring to the traditional definition of artists, writers, performers. You may not consider yourself a creative person, but if you had an idea for a business, that in itself is original thinking. If you lead a company, you will constantly be challenged to think of outside-the-box solutions to problems. The demands of running a business require creativity in how you position yourself in the market or differentiate yourself from your competitors, how you engage consumers, how you design products or package services. It requires original and independent thinking, so it's time to expand your view of who you are. Creativity comes in many forms.

I have found that, for me, alone time boosts creativity not only because I can let my mind wander but also because it allows me to actually tune in and listen to my inner voice and really pay attention to my thoughts. Human beings have an average of more than six thousand thoughts per day. It's impossible to pay attention to every single one of them, of course, but when you're constantly focused on other people – answering their questions or giving them direction or trying to attract their attention – you're even less likely to notice what's going on inside your own head. When you're entirely fixated on what your customers are thinking – whether they will like your product and how you can position it to be appealing to them – it's easy to forget to pay any mind to what *you're* thinking.

I really cherish the opportunity to tune in to my own thoughts. As much as I value other people's knowledge and expertise, at the end of the day I trust myself most. My instincts have served me quite well up to this point, and it's important to me that I don't get caught up in the noise of what I *should* do, or fall victim to following what everyone else is doing. As I've said throughout this book, you as the business owner and founder and visionary are the expert on your company; you have an inner voice that will lead you in the right direction, but you need to be able to hear it, and that's a skill in itself. Alone time helps cultivate intuition. It is where you can practise listening to that inner voice so that as your business gets busier and your head gets overcrowded with other people's input, you can zero in on your own opinions and instincts. That's how the idea to partner with Jacqui on The Pilates Class came to me. I was at home doing one of the online classes that she offered her existing clients on Instagram during the pandemic, and I just had this feeling. Something special was happening, and there was opportunity there. I'm probably not the only person who thought to themselves, *Wow, Jacqui is really incredible at this*. I mean, anyone who has taken her classes can tell she has a presence that jumps off the screen – it feels as if you're in her private studio, with a trainer standing beside you, even though you're in your bedroom or living room. But I was the only person who saw, or at least pursued, the business potential. That's in part because I'm obsessed with entrepreneurism – as I said in the Introduction, I would start fifty companies if I could, that's how much I love it – but also because I've trained myself to recognise the sparks of an idea that start off as a whisper.

Hearing the whispers

Big light-bulb moments sound pretty cool. It would be truly fantastic if every business idea came to us fully formed, with all the complicated logistics worked out and an entirely clear sense of what the final launched product or service will look like. But that's almost never how it happens. Usually, an idea starts out as a whisper. It might get louder and louder over time ... but also it might not. It might be a message that, if you don't pay attention, simply goes away. And even if it is the kind of whisper that eventually becomes a shout, the ability to tune in the first time, when it first comes to you, has a lot of value. That kind of attention could get you to market faster, or perhaps before someone else has the same thought. It will also give you time to meditate on the idea, to think it through and work out the complications before you feel that tug of 'I need to act now!'

Tuning in to the whispers ties back, in large part, to trust and confidence. We often underestimate our own thoughts. If, like me, you have no formal business education you might brush off the ideas that come to you. *What do I know?* you might be thinking. *I've never started a business. This idea is probably not even that great. Or if it is, someone else has probably tried and failed, otherwise it would already exist.* You need to have the confidence and trust in yourself to know that your ideas have merit, and if they lodge themselves in your mind and linger for a while, there's probably a reason. But, again, cultivating that kind of recognition and trust takes practice, and requires peace and quiet from time to time. I meditate nearly every day, and a big part of meditation is to recognise when thoughts enter your head and acknowledge them without judgement. It's not *Ugh, this idea is dumb* or even *Wow, this is brilliant!* It's about noticing and observing. *Huh, this whisper keeps coming to me. There must be a reason for that. Maybe I should pay attention.* Because maybe it's true that someone else has tried and failed, but that doesn't mean you will too. If you allow yourself time and space to think through your business idea without rushing it, you might come up with a different and more financially sound approach that will buy you more time to really build the business. You might have a different marketing angle. You might have a different company structure or manufacturing approach. The point is, you need to trust yourself and have confidence in your own ideas. Your inner voice should be louder and more powerful than any of the outside voices fighting to get in.

When I find myself doubting my inner voice (which, I'll admit, doesn't happen often – innate confidence has been helpful, but self-doubt occurs less over time when your intuition has repeatedly proven itself credible), I engage in a thought exercise to build myself up. Some people might suggest standing in front of a mirror and talking to yourself out loud, but I've found that closing your eyes and saying something in your head is even more powerful when you are intentional about it. If I have a thought I'm doubting, or a whisper that I'm not sure about, I sit quietly and I say that thing over and over. It's almost like a mantra, although in this case it's not about grounding myself but more about believing in myself. By repeating it in my head, and really focusing on the thought, it will grow stronger and I'll believe it. Whether the idea is an internal pep talk (*I can do this; I can lead a business*) or more specific and external (*This is a good idea; it has business potential; I should pursue it*), blocking out the outside noise and taking time to focus on my own thoughts is what helps me prioritise and trust my own thinking. It also helps with manifesting. After all, your thoughts become your reality, and it's something you can fine-tune. But it requires moments of quiet and solitude. And it requires practice. Sitting with your thoughts one time is better than none, but getting to a place where you can calm your mind and slow down your thinking and recognise the whispers and go deeper takes repetition and experience. Ideally, it's an everyday thing, not a once-in-a-while one.

My daily routine

I make sure to incorporate at least a few moments of solitude into my schedule every day, and as I write this book, most of it happens in the mornings. Waking up and immediately taking time to myself sets the tone for the day – if the first thing you do after opening your eyes is grab your phone and start responding to work emails (like I did for so many years), you're already off to the races. It can be hard to dial it back once you've checked in with colleagues and people know you're online. Not to mention the fact that jumping into the workday will likely get your nervous system amped up. You know the feeling – you read a work email and you immediately feel your heart or mind (or both) start racing. There's a sense of urgency as you jump into problem-solving mode. It might feel like a rush in the moment, because getting stuff done really can feel exciting and productive and badass, but it's not healthy for anyone to be running on overdrive all day. Constantly spiked adrenal and cortisol levels aren't great for your body's ability to function. Starting your day from a place of calm and balance, and prioritising things like meditation or fitness, will help establish a level-headed approach to whatever is thrown at you later. I've read books like *The 5 AM Club* by leadership expert Robin Sharma, which outline all the benefits of a holistic morning routine, because this is something that some of the most world-renowned executives and business owners take very seriously. I certainly don't wake up at 5 a.m. (although I did try it out for a while – not for me!), but I apply all the other ideologies of this concept, including incorporating movement, reflection and learning into my mornings.

One of the first things I do every day is make my bed. Gretchen Rubin, author of *The Happiness Project*, writes in the book about her 'secrets of adulthood'. One of the big ones? Outer order contributes to inner calm. I absolutely subscribe to this idea, which is why even when I'm working from home, which happens fairly often, it's important to me to make the bed, get the house organised, and get dressed and feel presentable. Even if I'm not going to see anyone, when I feel put together on the outside, it helps me feel that way on the inside too. But before I shower and get dressed, I do my best to get outside for a Pilates workout or at least a short walk – I always try to get the sun on my face first thing if I can – and then I do some quiet breathwork in order to calm my nervous system and get regulated for the day, and spend a few moments making notes in my gratitude journal. None of it takes a super long time – I spend less than ten minutes on the breathwork and the gratitude journal – but the return on investment is huge in terms of mental clarity and inner strength. These are the kinds of activities that will fill your cup, which you'll learn pretty quickly is a requirement when you are trying to give 110 per cent to your business and the people around you every day.

The first hour or two of my day really are about just me. I see my husband, of course, but as an entrepreneur himself, he acknowledges and respects my need for a calm entry into the day. Also, he's my life partner. My husband prioritises my health as much as I do, and the beauty of a healthy partnership is that you aren't a drain on each other's resources but a support system.

During the workday, I don't get a lot of alone time. It's the nature of the beast and I don't want to sit here and tell you to be both excessively obsessed and also spend your day focused on self-care – it's just not realistic. Your days will be busy and taxing if you're running a business. I try to do three to five minutes of breathwork in between meetings, especially in moments when I can feel myself getting edgy, and

I always practise the 20/20 rule I mentioned in the previous chapter (twenty minutes of focus, at least twenty seconds to step away). Towards the end of the day, I step away from the computer for a longer meditation practice (fifteen minutes rather than five). But, in truth, it's a pretty active schedule from when I start working at about 8 a.m. to when I stop around 5 or 6 p.m., which is why once I shut my computer for the day, I try to circle back to where I began: unplugged and focused on self-maintenance. Yes, if I get a work email or important text I respond, and sometimes I'm travelling or have other work obligations that make a quiet night harder to come by. But when I can, I make every effort to engage in non-tech related activities or hobbies, get outside again and put my phone away for the evening at a reasonable time. I find that when I can follow my own advice, I am more present for myself, my family and friends, and my company. I'm healthier, which means my relationships and career are healthier – and that's a big plus for any entrepreneur who needs at least a few years to get a company off the ground.

My daily schedule

6.30 a.m. Wake up, get out of bed
Wash face, brush teeth
Open the curtains and make my bed
Drink a glass of water
7 a.m. Go outside for a walk or workout
7.30 a.m. Eight minutes of breathwork to deregulate my nervous system
Five minutes on my gratitude journal
Shower, get dressed and ready for work

8.30 a.m. Start work
Follow the 20/20 rule throughout the day
Drink water regularly
12.30 p.m. Lunch break, fifteen to sixty minutes,
depending on the day
1 p.m. Back to work
3 p.m. Meditation, fifteen to twenty-five minutes,
depending on where I am
5 p.m. Short outdoor walk or break
6 p.m. Finish work
Take a bath with Epsom salts and essential oils
most nights
Cook or do another activity that gets me away from
technology
6.30 p.m. Eat dinner with my husband
8 p.m. Put my phone away for the night
Drink a cup of herbal tea
9.30 p.m. Get ready for bed
Skincare routine including essential oils like lavender oil,
which helps calms me after a long day
Journaling (if I couldn't get to it in the morning)
10 p.m. Sleep

Setting boundaries

Just because I know better doesn't mean I always do better, and establishing and holding boundaries is one area where I am definitely a work in progress. What do I mean by boundaries? They look different for everyone, but they might include saying no to additional responsibilities or social engagements or requests for your time and energy, or protecting your alone time (or simply your non-work time) by setting a hard-and-fast deadline for when you log off, like I mentioned earlier. Maybe you hold the line that you do not work on Sundays, and you're clear about that with colleagues and employees. Or maybe you have an hour or two of each day that you establish as unplugged time. That hour might be for your workout, or for a sit-down family dinner. What you do with your time will depend on your priorities and your life stage, but what matters is that you are clear with yourself and others. Ultimately, boundaries are about identifying what you need to feel healthy and like your best self, and then advocating for those needs without apology.

Holding boundaries doesn't mean being entirely inflexible. There will be times when you have to make exceptions, and other times when you have to expand or change them altogether. It also doesn't mean being mean or unhelpful. Many of us, women in particular, have been raised to say yes, yes, yes to whatever anyone needs of us, and saying no without offering a reason or an apology can feel scary. But the goal of creating whatever limits you set is to protect yourself from feeling overextended or taken advantage of, so that you are in better shape to lead and work and perform at a high level in the long run. And even if it may appear on the surface as if boundaries are largely established to protect you from others, what I've learned is that when you're an excessively obsessed entrepreneur, the most important thing about boundaries is that they protect you from yourself.

Take a regular weekday evening. As much as you know you want to unplug for a bit before bed each night, it's easy to get so caught up in work that you never quite log off until you are passed out at 11 p.m., long after you meant to stop working. But if you set yourself a boundary – say, no computers past 8 p.m.

or phone down an hour before bedtime – and generally hold firm, you are doing yourself a big favour. Back when Monday was the only business I was in charge of, I got pretty good at figuring out what I needed in order to maintain my sanity and sticking to it. Monday was finally operating like a well-oiled machine, which meant there were fewer demands on my time and it was easier to hold firm in terms of what I knew was best for me. Now that I'm running multiple businesses, two of which are still relatively young, it's not so easy. I want to give all my time and attention to both companies, because I love them and believe in them and feel confident that I know what's best for them, so I am constantly reminding myself that what's best for me, and in turn what's ultimately best for the companies, is if I maintain the boundaries that help protect my health – this has been a huge adjustment for me but also the best change I've ever made.

If reinforcing your own boundaries is hard for you, there are plenty of tech solutions that can help. You could block off time in your calendar so that no one can book calls or meetings during your 'protected' time. You can take advantage of screen time settings on your phone to block you out of certain apps, like social media after a certain length of time. On most smartphones, you can set a 'bedtime' or you can set reminders to get up and stretch or step away from the screen. At the very least, you can set your phone to 'do not disturb' mode so that you aren't constantly getting alerts when you're trying to sleep. The point is, if you have trouble defending your boundaries and protecting your alone time, you're not the only one. I'm right there with you. And accepting help in this regard isn't a weakness but a strength. Like any good business person, you know what you need to do, and you're enlisting the tools to make it happen.

13

Finding your purpose

If you can't figure out your purpose, figure out your passion. For your passion will lead you right into your purpose.

BISHOP T. D. JAKES

When I think about my career journey thus far, I picture a flowing river. I can see it clearly in my mind. One decision or opportunity leads to the next, and as I'm letting the current carry me, new ideas might appear that propel me in an unexpected direction, but I know I need to move along with the momentum. When a decision or new endeavour feels too hard, or if I'm resisting a change that seems inevitable, it's as if I'm holding on to a boulder, fighting the current and trying to stay in one place rather than going with the flow. It's an image that serves me, because when it feels like I'm too attached to an endeavour that isn't working, or the career moves I'm making don't feel natural (and if you pay attention to that inner voice as you move through your life, you can usually tell if something just *feels* right or if it feels forced), I can ask myself: 'Are you clinging to the boulder? Can you let go and let the river take you?'

The analogy works because movement equals growth, and growth is what leads to fulfilment. Staying in one place and never learning something new eventually gets boring, and no one who spends their days bored to death would describe themselves as fulfilled. You don't want to feel constantly overwhelmed and out of your depth, because that's a fast track to burnout, but a healthy amount of challenge is what eventually results in satisfaction and, ultimately, happiness. This analogy can also work with regard to your wellness routine and personal life. Do you feel like you're flowing in the right direction, or do things seem to be going wrong constantly? If the latter, maybe you're not letting go or trusting the process enough.

Different people have different success metrics, but I would caution you against tying your version of career and business success entirely to your financial outcome. Being excessively obsessed only really happens when you get non-monetary benefits from work. It's not success if you're miserable – even if you're rich and miserable. That's no one's lifelong dream. The dream of entrepreneurship might include financial gain but that's usually alongside happiness, enjoyment and fulfilment. The excessive obsession comes from the feeling that you are *called* to the work. That you have found your purpose and are working in that space, rather than trying to fit into a mould or serve a vision that someone else's company has created for you.

Forget about the price tag

The fulfilment that comes from finding your purpose – and actually being lucky enough to work towards it – is more valuable than any fortune you might earn from your business venture. I promise you this. Enjoying your work and feeling an overall sense of joy is worth making ten times less than you could while working your butt off and hating every second of it, or feeling constant stress or fear or exhaustion. (Even in a fulfilling job you probably won't be joyful every second of the day because, hello, this is real life, but you want to feel like 'I love my work' even if there are small parts of it that you could do without.) I know that might be hard to believe, or it might sound easy for me to say because my businesses are established and running at a profit. But of all the stories I've shared in this book, what brought me the most joy – and what was honestly the most fun in the moment – were the days when Devin and I were working on A Bikini A Day in our apartment. We weren't even making any money yet, but it was so empowering to be building something of our own and knowing, without question, that we could make it work. Really the only thing I ever hoped for was to be able to pay my bills, have a small amount of savings and not be financially stressed. Other people might have questioned us, and they did, but we believed in ourselves entirely. It was the first time I really felt like I was doing exactly what I was made for.

And the hardest memory? The days of long Covid, hands down. Yes, I was running two successful and financially viable businesses, but I would have traded it all for my health and happiness when I was at my lowest. There's an idea that money equals freedom, and yes, that's true to a degree. I am incredibly lucky to no longer have to worry about how I will pay the rent, or if I'll have enough left over for groceries. I am grateful for that every single day. But 'more money more problems' is an expression for a reason. As Monday, TPC and TBC get more successful, there are more eyes on us and more pressure. There's always another job to do and higher stakes attached to all of it. We are responsible for other people's livelihoods, there are probably people out there rooting for us to fail, and we have partners we would be letting down if things went south. But it's not either/or. You don't have to choose between being fulfilled and making money. There is a beautiful and balanced sweet spot where you can make a living and feel financially comfortable and internally fulfilled without the stress of running a mega-company, and for most of us that's the dream.

Remember, you will spend a huge portion of your waking hours at work. A 2023 report from the International Labour Organization, an agency of the UN, found that 'globally, over one-third of all workers are regularly working more than 48 hours per week'. It varies a bit by country: at the high end, workers in the US work, on average, 1,750 hours a year, while Germans, at the low end of the countries studied, worked 1,350 hours a year. And for entrepreneurs, that number is even higher. Conventional wisdom is that entrepreneurs work sixty hours a week – that's more than three thousand hours a year! If you're going to dedicate that much time to anything (and, to be clear, I don't think a sixty-hour week is particularly healthy, and I'll always promote working smarter rather than longer), you want to enjoy it. Even more than that, you want to feel like you are doing something meaningful, and that it contributes to your larger purpose.

Still, as is usually the case, it's not one size fits all. Everyone will feel fulfilled by something different. Growth is pretty universally correlated to fulfilment; money, on the whole, is not. It helps, absolutely, but it's not enough. A 2023 survey of multiple studies from more than one hundred countries and forty-four cultures, published in the *International Journal of Environmental Research and Public Health,* found that the major elements that determine happiness are wellbeing (physical, mental, emotional), work–life balance, relationships and self-care. Money might move the happiness needle in the moment – who doesn't love getting a raise or, even better, a windfall – but research shows it doesn't lead to greater fulfilment over time because we eventually return to our baseline level, whatever that is.

Aside from an overall sense of growth, each of us might find fulfilment in something different. For me, it's taking on and leading new projects. I love the excitement of venturing into the unknown. For someone else, fulfilment might be working on causes they believe in. And, for someone else again, it might be engaging in creative pursuits like writing or designing or performing. Businesses can be started in any of these areas and so many more. When we can actually make a living doing the thing that fulfils us, when you wake up feeling like you're doing what you're called to do – that's what I would call success.

Always come back to the mission

When you first establish your business, you will spend time thinking about your company's values. *What do you stand for? What customer needs are you solving for? Why is what you are doing important to you? What will drive how you operate as an employer?* You might lay out a mission statement. You may even have two versions: one that is customer-facing, about the mission behind your products and services; another for internal use, about what drives your company, how you want to lead and the conduct that is expected of all employees. Knowing what your business is about and being clear on your intention is the first step, but having the ability to check in with yourself and recognise when you've got caught up in the hamster wheel and lost sight of those driving values is just as important, if not more so. It's bound to happen – businesses grow and change at a rapid pace and you won't have time every day to evaluate if your every move is aligned with your values. You might get caught up in a deal and not realise until way down the line that the partner on the other end isn't the right fit. You could get so excited about the success of a product and pumping out more supply before you lose the momentum that you demand more of your employees and forget that you vowed to prioritise their work–life balance. None of this means you've become some kind of tyrannical CEO. That only happens when you refuse to re-evaluate or self-reflect, or you reject any efforts towards course-correcting.

I try to engage in a monthly or quarterly check-in for my businesses, where I look at what we're working on and how we're operating, to be sure that everything we're doing can be traced back to our original intentions. At The Pilates Class, we've had moments where we launch an apparel line, for example, and because it's new and customers are excited, all of us in the company get caught up in the promotion even though apparel is really not what we're about. Our values are about wellness – relieving ourselves of physical tension and mental stress and treating our bodies with the love and care they deserve. Cute clothes are a fun extra, but they aren't part of our core values and as the leader of the business it's my job to say, 'Hey guys, we've shifted our focus too much to something that's not a part of our brand pillars.' It's easy to get distracted, so as a business leader it's on you to redirect the focus.

Staying true to your values is as important for you individually as it is for your company. Just as you should know what your company stands for, you should also have an idea of what *you* are about. How do you want to lead? What kind of persona do you want to present to your employees and the world? What are the beliefs that drive you and the values you want to embody as a business owner and entrepreneur? Once you have those answers, you need to be sure you practise what you preach. Even the most well-intentioned, kind-hearted person can get off track, and being overworked or tired or stressed makes it even easier to get caught up and lose your way. Actively checking in to be sure you are staying true to your intention will keep you accountable. For example, one of your personal commandments might be to keep a positive attitude with yourself and others. A check-in where you really look at your own behaviours might uncover that you've been pretty negative lately, either in your own internal self-talk or by being overly critical with your team. Like me, you might believe in following the momentum but realise that you have instead been clinging to the boulder, resisting change or movement. Being honest with yourself and making changes in the right direction is hard but admirable. No one's perfect, but being able to see where you've strayed will get you one step closer.

What I've learned over time is that if you don't remain humble, life has a way of humbling you. It happened to me, that's for sure. Lying on the couch for weeks on end because I could barely move was a real reminder that I had lost sight of some of my personal values – like prioritising my health and setting boundaries to protect my peace. On the other hand, I truly believe that if you are living your beliefs and staying true to your purpose, everything else – the career, the fulfilment, the joy – will fall into place.

Conclusion
Embrace the unknown

If you're here with me at the end of this book, then you have probably either started a business, are seriously considering starting a business or are contemplating pursuing a big career move. There is change and adventure in your near future, whether it's a new job or business endeavour, or maybe a promotion or side hustle. After all, if you're the kind of person who is excessively obsessed and likes to think big, you probably can't sit around idly for long. But even still – despite being armed with all the knowledge offered in these pages – you might feel a tinge of fear. Doing something new comes with a lot of uncertainty. Before I wrote this book, friends who had business ideas would approach me all the time to ask for my two cents, and I would say the same thing to them that I will say to you right now: I am so excited for you! And even a tiny bit jealous! Going through a major change – even those that on the surface seem negative, like a break-up or getting fired – is thrilling to me, because there's so much opportunity in the unknown and it puts you on the path towards what is really meant to be.

As far as I'm concerned, the best part of life is not knowing what comes next and being in that stage where literally anything could happen. I still have so much more I want to accomplish with my businesses – I'm a long way from 'done' – yet nothing compares to the earliest days of my career, when I had absolutely no idea, not a clue, where I would be today. There was so much potential, the possibilities truly seemed endless. Just remembering that feeling sends chills down my arms and puts a smile on my face. And the fact that you picked up this book and wanted to learn from someone else's business experience – that alone tells me that big things are coming for you. It may not be tomorrow. You might have worked your way through these chapters only to decide that you aren't ready, that you need more time to explore your idea before you jump into starting a company, or you want to focus on growing in the job you're in currently. That's a great discovery, and smart thinking. I absolutely support and encourage taking all the time you need. But if the excessively obsessed mindset is swirling for you, I think you might surprise yourself. Once you are tuned in to that frequency, you'll notice that you look at the world differently. You are more in touch with your purpose, and everything feels like it could be an idea. And because you are more centred and tuned in to your inner voice, you will be able to distinguish between the inklings that provoke a 'Hmm, maybe that could be something' and those that scream 'Yes, this is what I've been waiting for. This is what I am *meant for.*'

Hold on tight to those ideas and know that they came to you for a reason. When you find the career pursuit that uncovers your purpose and makes you feel fulfilled, the work may be hard and demanding, and the mental ticker tape may wake you up in the middle of the night, but in the midst of all that effort you will feel settled in and comfortable. When you find your calling, it's not unlike finding that just-right bathing suit ... the perfect fit.

RESOURCES

Glossary

Your business vocabulary will expand with your experience, but here are some key terms that are helpful to know, especially in online retail or services.

Average order value (AOV): The average amount a customer spends each time they place an online order. The formula to find the AOV is total revenue divided by number of orders.

Churn rate: The rate at which customers stop doing business with a brand, or the number of subscribers who cancel or unsubscribe. The formula to find your churn rate is to divide lost customers by total number of customers at the start of whatever time period you are measuring.

Click-through rate (CTR): The percentage of people who see a page, email or advertisement and actually click on it. CTR measures engagement, and can be found by dividing the number of clicks by the number of individuals who saw the content (otherwise known as impressions).

Customer relationship management (CRM): The process of managing and tracking interactions with current and potential customers, usually through CRM software (like Salesforce). The goal of CRM is to gather data about customers in order to improve relationships with them and retain them.

Direct to consumer (D2C): A digital business model in which companies sell their products direct to consumers, without using third-party retailers.

EBITDA: This stands for earnings before interest, taxes, depreciation and amortisation. It is a formula to measure a company's financial health and ability to generate cash flow, and is useful for potential investors or for your own understanding of your business's potential. Your EBITDA is the sum of your business's net income, interest, tax, depreciation and amortisation.

Key performance indicators (KPIs): Your specific KPIs will be different for different projects, but they are generally quantifiable indicators of success, like number of sales in a quarter or number of new subscribers in a month. If you don't hit your KPIs, it's an indicator that a project has not met its objectives.

Lifetime customer value (LCV): The total revenue a company can expect from a single customer throughout that customer's entire relationship with the company, determined by first multiplying the average total order amount by the average number of purchases per year, and then multiplying that number by the average customer lifespan.

Omnichannel: The integration of multiple channels (for example, websites, apps, social media, email) so that the customer shopping experience is easy and unified across all channels.

Return on assets (ROA): A measure of a company's profitability in relation to its total assets, ROA is used to measure how efficiently a company uses its own assets to generate profit. The formula for ROA is the company's net income divided by its total assets.

Return on investment (ROI): A formula for measuring the success of an investment, ROI is calculated by dividing the profit by the original cost of an investment.

Return rate: The percentage of products sold that are returned.

Returning customer rate: The percentage of customers who make at least two purchases within any given time period.

Search engine optimisation (SEO): A strategy to make a website more search-engine friendly, so that it ranks higher in Google and other search engine searches.

Appendix A:

Sample budgeting sheet

This sample budgeting sheet includes fields for all of Monday's revenue streams and business expenses. Depending on your business, you may have more, fewer or different fields, but the top-line categories – revenue, costs of goods sold, operating expenses and operating income – will be pretty much the same.

	Jan	Feb	Mar	Apr	May	Jun	Jul	Aug	Sep	Oct	Nov	Dec	Total
Revenue													
Sponsorship Income													0.00
Merchandise Sales													0.00
Shipping Income													0.00
Discounts													0.00
Sales Returns													0
Total Revenue (Net)	–	–	–	–	–	–	–	–	–	–	–	–	–
Cost of Goods Sold													
Inventory – Beginning													0
Inventory – End													0
Warehousing													0
Warehouse Supplies													0
Samples													0
Labels and Packaging													0
Merchant Account Fees													0
Shipping – Customer Orders													0
Shipping – Inventory													0
Shipping – Duties													0
Total Cost of Goods Sold	0	0	0	0	0	0	0	0	0	0	0	0	0
Gross Margin	–	–	–	–	–	–	–	–	–	–	–	–	–

	Jan	Feb	Mar	Apr	May	Jun	Jul	Aug	Sep	Oct	Nov	Dec	Total
Gross Margin %	0%	0%	0%	0%	0%	0%	0%	0%	0%	0%	0%	0%	0%
Operating Expenses													
General Operating Expenses													
Merchant Fees													0
Rent Expenses													0
Postage and Shipping													0
Office Supplies													0
Telephone Expenses													0
Repairs and Maintenance													0
Insurance Expenses													0
Storage													0
Computer and Internet Expenses													0
Total General Operating Expenses	0	0	0	0	0	0	0	0	0	0	0	0	0
Advertising and Promotion													
PR Services													0
Digital Marketing													0
Website Costs													0

	Jan	Feb	Mar	Apr	May	Jun	Jul	Aug	Sep	Oct	Nov	Dec	Total
Advertising													0
Paid Partnerships													0
Content Creation													0
Charitable Contributions													0
Event Expenses													0
Graphic Designer													0
Photography/Videography													0
Total Advertising and Promotion	0	0	0	0	0	0	0	0	0	0	0	0	0
Personnel Expenses													
Salaries and Wages													0
Admin Staff													0
Payroll Processing Fees													0
Health Insurance													0
Payroll Taxes													0
Total Personnel Expenses	0	0	0	0	0	0	0	0	0	0	0	0	0
Professional Fees													
Accounting													0

	Jan	Feb	Mar	Apr	May	Jun	Jul	Aug	Sep	Oct	Nov	Dec	Total
Consultants	0												0
Legal		0	0	0	0	0	0	0	0	0	0	0	0
Total Professional Fees	0												0
Travel and Entertainment													
Automobile Expenses													0
Travel Expenses													0
Meals and Entertainment													0
Total Travel and Entertainment	0	0	0	0	0	0	0	0	0	0	0	0	0
Total Operating Expenses	0	0	0	0	0	0	0	0	0	0	0	0	0
Operating Income (EBITDA)	0	0	0	0	0	0	0	0	0	0	0	0	0
EBITDA %	0%	0%	0%	0%	0%	0%	0%	0%	0%	0%	0%	0%	0%

Appendix B

Sample marketing calendar (established company)

This is a top-line marketing initiative outline that can be shared with the team, cross-referenced across departments and used for year-over-year analysis. It's also a great document to reference in team meetings so that everyone is aligned on marketing priorities. Most businesses can utilise a general plan like this one, which we used for Monday's summer 2023 season. If your business is smaller, your calendar may only be half a page long with one or two initiatives per month (see Appendix C), but the template will still be the same.

SU23:

APRIL

- APRIL 6: TEASE SUMMER DROP 1
- APRIL 10: SUMMER '23 LAUNCH – LEMONGRASS CRINKLE, ISLAND AURA, CHILI PEPPER
  - NEW STYLES: SANTA CRUZ SHORTS; KAUAI TOP; KAUAI BOTTOM; CLOVELLY ONE PIECE

- APRIL 12: NEW STYLES FEATURE
- APRIL 17: BTS OF CAMPAIGN SHOOT + GUIDE TO TULUM
- APRIL 19: DROP 1 INFLUENCER FEATURE
- APRIL 20: TOP 100 VIPS GET EXCLUSIVE LOOK AT SUMMER COLLECTION
- APRIL 21: CHILI PEPPER FEATURE
- APRIL 24: HUSK & IVORY/BLACK (TWO TONE) LAUNCH
    - NEW STYLES: SAUSALITO ONE PIECE, AZORES TOP

- APRIL 26: HUSK FEATURE
- APRIL 28: CAPRI WAVE EARLY ACCESS FOR VIPS

MAY

- MAY 1: CAPRI WAVE & BLACK CRINKLE LAUNCH
    - NEW STYLES: LAGUNA TOP; BIMINI DRESS; KOKOMO DRESS

- MAY 3: DRESS FEATURE
- MAY 5: CAPRI WAVE FEATURE
- MAY 8: FUCHSIA BERRY LAUNCH IN SWIM & BEACHWEAR + PEARL SHIMMER RESTOCK
- MAY 9: PEARL SHIMMER RESTOCK FEATURE (EMAIL)
- MAY 15: ANNOUNCE/TEASE GROVE POP-UP SHOP
- MAY 15: RESTOCK: NEWPORT DRESS & CAPE MAY SKIRT – IVORY CROCHET AND HAMILTON ISLAND SWEATER & PANT – (NO EMAIL)

- **MAY 15: RIDE THE WAVE LAUNCH & VALENCIA BAG SMALL & VALENCIA BAG LARGE LAUNCH**
- MAY 16: RIDE THE WAVE FOCUS EMAIL + BEACHWEAR RESTOCK IN EMAIL
- MAY 16: SHOPIFY PARTNERSHIP ENTREPRENEUR GIVEAWAY
- MAY 17: GROVE ONLINE BOOKING OPENS
- **MAY 22: BIRD OF PARADISE & JUNGLE LAUNCH**
- **CHARITABLE INITIATIVE – JUNGLE**
  - **ONE TREE PLANTED FOR EVERY ORDER**

- MAY 24: JUNGLE FOCUS
- MAY 25–29: MEMORIAL DAY 20% OFF FULL WEBSITE. CODE: LONGWEEKEND20
- **MAY 29: TWO-TONE RESTOCK ALL STYLES**
- **MAY 30: CITRUS CROCHET LAUNCH**
  - CHARITABLE INITIATIVE – FLAVIANA MATATA FOUNDATION

- **MAY 31: NAVY SHIMMER EXCLUSIVE EARLY ACCESS LAUNCH + POP-UP OPEN**

JUNE

- JUNE 2: SHOP CASH GIVEAWAY
- **JUNE 5: NAVY SHIMMER, BRIDAL WHITE (SWIM) & TRUE WHITE CROCHET DRESSES**
  - NEW STYLES: COZUMEL DRESS & MONTEGO DRESS IN WHITE OPEN CROCHET

- **JUNE 7: BRIDAL COLLECTION (TRUE WHITE) FEATURE (EMAIL)**
- JUNE 7: GROVE FIT WEEK

- **JUNE 12: BLACK CRINKLE RESTOCK & ST TROPEZ BAG LARGE LAUNCH**
- JUNE 15: DREAM BLUE RESTOCK
- JUNE 13–20: GOLDEN VACATION PARTNERSHIP GIVEAWAY
- JUNE 13–17: ST TROPEZ INFLUENCER 4 – NIGHT SLEEPOVER
  - JUNE 14: TASH'S LAST SPLASH POOL PARTY ST TROPEZ

- **JUNE 18: GROVE STYLING WEEK**
- JUNE 19: SIGNATURE PUSH OUR SIGNATURE SCULPTING FABRIC (USE RETRO STYLE PHOTOS FROM TULUM)
- **JUNE 21: NEW PREMIUM RIB PIECES LAUNCH, TASH EVERYDAY ESSENTIALS**
- SILVER LAKE TOP – WHITE
  - MARINA DEL REY TOP – WHITE
  - LAUREL CANYON TOP – WHITE
  - BEVERLY HILLS TOP – WHITE
  - BEL AIR BOTTOM – WHITE
  - LAUREL CANYON TOP – BLACK
  - BEVERLY HILLS TOP – BLACK
  - SILVER LAKE TOP – BLACK

- JUNE 22: ST TROPEZ EVENT EMAIL
- **JUNE 22: GROVE FABRIC WEEK**
- **JUNE 26: HUSK GEO LAUNCH & NEW HUSK CRINKLE BEACHWEAR AND HAMPTONS KNITWEAR DRESS**
- JUNE 28: HUSK GEO FEATURE

Appendix C

Sample marketing calendar (small company)

In the earliest days of your business, you probably won't have weekly launches or nearly as many events or giveaways as the example in Appendix B. Here's a sample marketing calendar for a fictional small dog grooming company in NYC.

NYC DOG GROOMING PARLOUR
COMPANY SIX-MONTH MARKETING OVERVIEW

Q1
JANUARY
WEEKS 1–4: REFER A FRIEND PROMOTION – FREE DOG BOWL WHEN YOU REFER A FRIEND
JAN 1: IN-STORE CAMPAIGN AND SOCIAL CONTENT SHOOT; MONTHLY NEWSLETTER SENT OUT TO DATABASE
JAN 2: LAUNCH EVENT: DOGGY COCKTAILS – BRING YOUR FURRY FRIEND, PUPCAKES FOR ALL
JAN 12: PRESS DAY – FREE DOG WASH + GROOMING FOR ALL PRESS CONTACTS
JAN 20: INSTAGRAM REEL: HOW WE PAMPER OUR PUPS

FEBRUARY
WEEK 4: LOCAL MAILBOX FLYER DROP
FEB 1: INSTAGRAM REEL: HAIR STYLES BY DOG BREED
FEB 2: MONTHLY NEWSLETTER SENT OUT
TO DATABASE
FEB 22: PETA FUNDRAISING EVENT IN NEARBY PARK

MARCH
MARCH 3: MONTHLY NEWSLETTER SENT OUT
TO DATABASE
MARCH 14: INSTAGRAM REEL TUTORIAL: TOUR OF OUR
GROOMING SPACE
MARCH 16: FREE PUPCAKE WITH EVERY
WASH THIS WEEK
MARCH 30: INSTAGRAM REEL TUTORIAL: DAY IN THE
LIFE OF OUR STAFF

Q2
APRIL
WEEKS 1–4: FACEBOOK ADVERTISING
CAMPAIGN TRIAL
APRIL 3: MONTHLY NEWSLETTER SENT OUT
TO DATABASE
APRIL 5: SOCIAL MEDIA GIVEAWAY WITH LOCAL VET –
WIN A FREE GROOMING SESSION
APRIL 7: INSTAGRAM REEL TUTORIAL: AT-HOME
GROOMING TIPS FOR YOUR PUP
APRIL 11: 25% OFF DOG WASH FOR
INTERNATIONAL PET DAY

MAY
MAY 2: TEAM BUILDING – LUNCH AND DOG WALK
MAY 3: MONTHLY NEWSLETTER SENT OUT

TO DATABASE

MAY 15: INSTAGRAM REEL TUTORIAL: OUR FAVOURITE GROOMING LOOKS SINCE OPENING

MAY 20: BOOK TWO SESSIONS AND GET ONE FREE – THIS WEEK ONLY!

MAY 21: *GOOD MORNING AMERICA* DOGGY FEATURE WITH OUR FOUNDER

JUNE

WEEK 2: LOCAL NYC BILLBOARD

JUNE 3: MONTHLY NEWSLETTER SENT OUT TO DATABASE

JUNE 20: INSTAGRAM REEL TUTORIAL: PUPPY TRAINING TIPS FROM OUR FAVOURITE TRAINER

JUNE 25: SHARE OUR FAVOURITE DOG-WALKING PLAYLIST ON SOCIAL MEDIA

Appendix D

Sample branding document

No matter how small a brand is, I always create a branding document to help me construct a marketing plan that makes sense. This is where I outline the information about the brand itself: what our message is, why we believe in it, what it does in simple terms and in a longer explanation. What are some quotes or taglines you can use that are unique to your brand? Are there branding opportunities in the functionality of your brand? (For example, you'll see that we categorised our TPC classes as 'chill', 'satisfying' and 'intense', which became a big part of our branding. Now we create brand schedules, challenges and even events based on these categories.) While your company might have different branding needs, the subsections below – including one-liners, social media opportunities, what your brand is and the core messaging – are a good place to start.

THE PILATES CLASS
One class, every 'body'!

THE CATEGORIES:

I'M IN THE MOOD FOR …

A CHILL CLASS
A 'GO EASY ON ME' CLASS

A SATISFYING CLASS
AN 'I JUST WANT TO FEEL GOOD' CLASS

AN INTENSE CLASS
A 'KICK MY BUTT, I NEED THIS' CLASS

ONE-LINERS:

THE PILATES CLASS – The only one you'll need
Get #ThePilatesClassBody

'Having "The Pilates Class Body" means you will feel
stronger, longer and leaner but also feel relief of physical
tension and mental stress.'

'I want my clients to set a new standard for their body and
what it deserves – to treat it with love and care because
confidence and beauty starts from within.'

'Haven't you ever noticed that Pilates teachers have the
best posture?'

'Pilates is one of the most transformative practices that you can do for your body and helps you to create sustainable and lasting change.'

'Unique approach.'

'Low-impact, high-repetition movements that will lengthen and tone but also give that deep burn in all the right places.'

'Whether Pilates is second nature to you, or if you're a beginner, a mum, business professional or all of the above ... The Pilates Class is for you.'

SOCIAL MEDIA

HASHTAGS:

#ThePilatesClassBody
#ThePilatesClassMethod
#TPCmembers
#TPCglow

THE PILATES CLASS METHOD

Jacqui Kingswell on why I created TPC:

The Pilates Class Method is something I personally created from movement and fitness of all kinds, which is a big part of my life. We utilise a series of low-impact, high-repetition movements to tone and lengthen your muscles. What is unique about this method is that we incorporate all different

types of movement, dance, boxing and cardio, as well
as traditional Pilates moves, into the classes. The most
important thing is that you learn to apply your 'Pilates
principles' and techniques to every move, which means you
are maximising the results. You will also feel the restorative
benefits from doing the Pilates Class method correctly and in
a way that serves your body.

I really wanted to create one class that is for every 'body',
not just every person but every body type, low fitness levels,
Pilates pros, men, women, pre- and postnatal: anyone that
wants to do the classes can find a level that works for them.
No matter what your goal is, you essentially wouldn't need
any other workout or class to achieve it because we are
incorporating it all.

Our approach is very holistic and that is the biggest change
that our members share with us once they join the platform,
that for the first time they feel connected to their body and
what it needs; they are listening to what it has to say and
giving it the love it deserves. Everyone that joins the platform
sets a new standard for their body and mind, and that makes
me so happy.

We offer three different levels – chill, satisfying and intense –
and you will most likely utilise every level throughout different
stages of your life. The best thing about Pilates is you can do
it for the rest of your life and the practice is almost addictive
and becomes a part of who you are and your daily routine.
Once you connect with your practice you will never be able
to imagine your life without it. The Pilates Class method
benefits you in all aspects of your life; it grounds you, helps
you to think positively and be kind to yourself; it brings you

confidence and consideration, not only for yourself but for others. It really is a beautiful practice to have in your life.

The amazing thing about Pilates in general is that it is scientifically proven to be beneficial in so many ways. It increases energy levels, helps with physical and mental stress, boosts your immunity and the list goes on. If you were to speak to any physio about what movement is the most restorative and beneficial for your body they would say Pilates – it improves posture, prevents injury, and increases your strength, balance and flexibility.

Something that makes me so happy every single day is seeing our members interact. We have created this beautiful community of positive and inspiring men and women all over the world that open up to one another, connect, share their honest feelings and hardships, and genuinely feel like they are a part of something that brings them happiness. I feel like a member of the community and love being a part of the conversation; I have definitely had a few laughs and tears from reading what others have shared.

WHAT TO EXPECT FROM A TPC CLASS

During the class you might experience a nice burn in targeted areas, but afterwards you can expect to feel really lengthened, energised and open.

Another great benefit you can expect from a Pilates workout is feeling really in tune with your mind and body and how it feels before and after the class.

HOW OFTEN JACQUI RECOMMENDS PRACTISING PILATES

The main thing is to listen to your body and how it is feeling – every day is different and every 'body' is different. The Pilates Class teaches you to tune in to your body, to listen to it and what it needs. This is one of The Pilates Class's fundamental practices.

We offer two weekly schedules on the platform, chill–satisfying and satisfying–intense, depending on what your goal is and how intense you would like your week to be.

For beginners, I recommend two to three classes per week combined with a thirty-minute walk. For a more intense workout I recommend four to five classes per week combined with a thirty-minute walk.

You don't need to feel exhausted after working out for it to be effective. Working out should make you feel energised, open and light.

PILATES IS SCIENTIFICALLY PROVEN TO:

- improve your memory and train your brain
- increase core and body strength
- improve posture, balance and flexibility
- prevent injuries
- decrease back pain
- promote deeper muscle activation, which means better function of the nervous system
- release mental stress and physical tension

- improve creativity
- increase energy and mood levels
- allow control of emotions by focusing on breathing
- help release emotional tension
- enhance body awareness
- boost immunity
- teach you self-love and confidence.

IMPORTANCE OF THE BREATH IN PILATES

Breath is so important in Pilates classes. It is the foundation of the core and one's fluidity in movement. Within the exercises, you activate and control your breath first, before performing any exercise. The controlled breathing activates the core and then the movement begins. In doing this, you get so much more out of the workout and a deeper connection with your body.

ORIGIN

Origin of Pilates
Pilates was created in the 1920s by Joseph Pilates, a German physical trainer, for the purpose of rehabilitation. Some of the first people treated by Pilates were soldiers returning from war, and dancers. It is a type of exercise focused on improving flexibility, strength and body awareness. Pilates focuses on really controlled movements, traditionally using body weight and resistance.

Origin of TPC
When entrepreneur and celebrity influencer Natasha Oakley

first began practising Pilates with Jacqui Kingswell, she instantly recognised Jacqui's classes were unlike any other she'd ever been a part of. As a former professional dancer, Jacqui's approach to Pilates is both unique and whole as she finds the balance between strength and movement. Having trained in Pilates for most of her life, to complement her rigorous dance training, she knew the restorative benefits Pilates had. As Jacqui's passion for Pilates grew, so did her following and influence in the fitness industry, leading to the organic transition to Pilates instructor and decision to partner with experienced businesswoman, Natasha. The Pilates Class launched during the pandemic, with a concentrated effort to be both financially and physically accessible to all. The TPC method is a unique approach to technique, posture and awareness. Jacqui and Natasha's combined influence in the health and fitness industry grew The Pilates Class from a passion project to a successful business with a tight-knit Pilates community, gaining the recognition of powerhouse publications like *Forbes*, *Vogue*, *Business Insider*, POPSUGAR and *Marie Claire*.

ABOUT THE PILATES CLASS

The Pilates Class is an online, technique-focused Pilates studio that can be used anywhere in the world. Created to transform the traditional approach to online fitness programmes, TPC's emphasis is on creating an online space and community where everyone, from stay-at-home moms to business professionals, can feel like they have the support and flexibility to incorporate health and fitness into their lifestyle.

The Pilates Class offers a wide range of restorative,

low-impact practices: from Pilates, barre, cardio and strength, to stretch, prenatal, postnatal and mindfulness classes. No matter where you are, what time it is or how active you feel, members can log on to the platform and find a class that brings them back to their mind and body.

WHY THE PILATES CLASS?

FLEXIBILITY isn't just what you'll gain but what we'll offer you in terms of fitting fitness into your schedule and routine.

STRENGTH is a given in most fitness classes, but at The Pilates Class we care about mental strength just as much as physical strength.

COMMUNITY can mean the difference between sticking to your classes or not – at TPC not only are we your community, but our members support one another throughout the journey.

UNDERSTANDING isn't easy to come by via digital fitness platforms, but Jacqui always finds a way to connect with and encourage her members in her classes.

INNOVATION is par for the course at TPC as we continuously strive to modify and create with the feedback we receive from members.

LOGOS

THE PILATES CLASS

THE
PILATES
CLASS

TPCkitchen

THE PILATES CLASS
by Jacqui Kingswell

Acknowledgements

The story of how this book came about relates back to many of the lessons from this book: don't be scared of the big publisher, because there may be someone there that believes in you! I want to thank Matt Crossey for being that person for me.

In 2017, I spoke on a 'women in business' panel at Soho House, Miami, where Matt, his lovely wife, Kate, and their daughter, Fleur, happened to be in the audience. Kate was in fashion and Matt in publishing and they visited Swim Week every year for Kate's work. Matt approached me on the beach saying he admired what I was doing in my career and that his daughter was also a fan. I saw the family every year at Swim Week. Meanwhile, I was manifesting the idea that I wanted my next challenge to be writing a book, about business, for women. A couple of years later, Matt was working at one of the UK's largest publishing firms and he reached out. He had pitched the idea of a book to the editor and she was interested in hearing more. Matt loved the idea that his daughter Fleur, who was ten at the time, could read my book one day and be inspired in her own career. I typed up my synopsis: 'What bikinis taught me about business.' The editor turned it down, but to me that was not a no, it was a 'not right now'. I could tell it was too early in my career and that at the perfect time the opportunity would come back my way.

Four years later, in 2022, I was in the midst of my Covid health nightmare, so I decided to skip Miami Swim Week to spend some downtime on a holiday in Spain. I was so sad to miss out, and having serious FOMO watching my team on the ground, but I knew it was the right choice for my health. Funnily enough, it turned out Matt, Kate and Fleur didn't go to Miami that year either – they were also in Spain! I ran into them at my favourite café in Ibiza, and was so happy to see them. Fleur was a teenager now. Matt mentioned he had been meaning to reach out; he was now with a new publisher who was forward-thinking and modern in her approach. Soon, he mentioned the concept of my book to Jillian Young, Little, Brown's Publishing Director, and she was very interested. Two weeks later we met in London and signed a contract for my first book. The name came about in the pitch meeting, after I told Jillian and Matt that for any business to be truly successful you have to be excessively obsessed with it. Who would have thought meeting Matt six years ago would have led to me creating this book today? But that is really just how it works.

I want to say a big thank you to Matt and Kate Crossey for asking me to write this book for their daughter Fleur.

Thank you to Jillian for having the vision for this book and believing in my ability to create it based on my own experiences.

A big thank you also to Rachel Bertsche for working with me on the pages of this book. I will always be grateful to you for helping me find my voice as a writer – there's no one I would have rather worked with on this project.

I also want to thank some of my mentors over the years,

who have always been there to give me advice or help me in any way. Melissa Odabash, the original supermodel swimwear designer, you were a huge inspiration to me early in my career and still are to this day. Jeff Abrams, founder of RAILS clothing, you have been a fountain of knowledge and always been so forthcoming with any learnings you thought could help me. Frasier Lipton, a friend since we first collaborated in our A Bikini A Day days, you and your family have always been there for Devin and me – we've been on this career journey together in many ways! Raissa Gerona, you are a boss and you have been supportive of my career and inspiring in more ways than you know. To my friend Harry Morton, who is now in heaven, your words of encouragement and interest in my career were always a huge driving force behind my confidence in business and I miss them very much.

To my father, Guy Oakley, thank you for always manifesting my success and for advertising my brands to everyone you can, even strangers on the street! I'm sure a part of why I am successful is purely because you believed in me. To my mother, Lynette Laming, my aspirations to become a businesswoman started from my youngest years, watching and listening to you in business everyday.

To my husband, Theodore Chambers, thank you for never holding me back and for always being on the sidelines cheering me on. I also am grateful that you inspired me to expand my knowledge of business and finance in so many ways.

Thank you to my amazing teams and especially long-time team members, Ahna Tillmans, Shannon Owens and Brittany Gallagher. You guys have always believed in me and my vision and worked tirelessly to see it come true.

To my business partner, Jacqui Kingswell, thank you for inspiring me to have a whole new perspective on wellness. I couldn't imagine my life without you as my Pilates trainer let alone without the amazing business we have built.

The biggest thank you goes to my business partner and best friend, Devin Brugman. It would be impossible to find a friendship and partnership as strong and as inspiring as ours. I count myself lucky every single day to have met you and know that the biggest contributor to my confidence and success as a businesswoman has been having you by my side through it all.